Sorting Machines

Sorting Machines

The Reinvention of the Border in the 21st Century

Steffen Mau

Translated by Nicola Barfoot

polity

Originally published in German as *Sortiermaschinen: Die Neuerfindung der Grenze im 21. Jahrhundert* ©Verlag C. H. Beck oHG, München 2021

Excerpt from *Refugee Conversations* ©Bertolt Brecht, 2016, Methuen Drama, an imprint of Bloomsbury Publishing Plc.

This English edition ©Polity Press, 2023

Polity Press
65 Bridge Street
Cambridge CB2 1UR, UK

Polity Press
111 River Street
Hoboken, NJ 07030, USA

ISBN-13: 978-1-5095-5434-8
ISBN-13: 978-1-5095-5435-5 (paperback)

A catalogue record for this book is available from the British Library.

Library of Congress Control Number: 2022934728

Typeset in 11 on 13pt Sabon
by Fakenham Prepress Solutions, Fakenham, Norfolk NR21 8NL
Printed and bound in the UK by TJ Books Limited

The publisher has used its best endeavours to ensure that the URLs for external websites referred to in this book are correct and active at the time of going to press. However, the publisher has no responsibility for the websites and can make no guarantee that a site will remain live or that the content is or will remain appropriate.

Every effort has been made to trace all copyright holders, but if any have been overlooked the publisher will be pleased to include any necessary credits in any subsequent reprint or edition.

For further information on Polity, visit our website:
politybooks.com

MIX
Paper from
responsible sources
FSC® C013056

The passport is the noblest part of a human being. Nor does it come into the world in such a simple way as a human being. A human being can come about anywhere, in the most irresponsible manner and with no proper reason at all, but not a passport. That's why a passport will always be honoured, if it's a good one, whereas a person can be as good as you like, and still no one takes any notice.

Bertold Brecht[1]

[1] Bertold Brecht, excerpt from *Refugee Conversations*, trans. Romy Fursland, ed. and intro. by Tom Kuhn © Bertolt Brecht, 2016, Methuen Drama, an imprint of Bloomsbury Publishing plc., p. 8.

Contents

Acknowledgements

This book is intended to inspire debate about territorial borders and border control in the age of globalization. It is compact and concise, focusing on the essentials, but it also draws on my own research projects and on broader research contexts in which I have been active in recent years. Among other things, it uses data collected and analysed within the framework of a project which I led at the University of Bremen (2007–14): 'From the Container to the Open State? Border Regime Changes and the Mobility of Persons', in the DFG Collaborative Research Centre 597, 'Transformations of the State'. In the context of this project, we primarily explored changing border policies in liberal states and developed a dataset on global changes in visa waivers. Fabian Gülzau, Lena Laube, Sonja Wrobel, Christof Roos and Heike Brabandt contributed significantly to this study. Since 2018, I have been leading a project in Berlin, 'Die Grenzen der Welt. Prozesse von De- und Rebordering in globaler Perspektive' ('The Borders of the World: Processes of Debordering and Rebordering from a Global Perspective'). This is based in Collaborative Research Centre 1265, 'Re-Figuration of Spaces', funded by the Deutsche Forschungsgemeinschaft

(DFG, German Research Foundation; project number 290045248). Here the focus is on the infrastructures of territorial borders. For this project we have developed a dataset containing all land borders worldwide and typologizing their border architectures. We are also conducting more in-depth case studies on four fortified borders: between Serbia and Hungary, the US and Mexico, Morocco and Algeria, and India and Pakistan. Fabian Gülzau and Kristina Korte are responsible for the implementation of the project and the empirical survey, and I would like to thank them for their many stimulating contributions. I am also grateful to be able to include findings from the project in this book. Special thanks go to my colleagues from the research unit 'Borders' – in particular Jessica Gienow-Hecht, Gülay Çağlar, Jürgen Gerhards, Christian Volk and Gwendolyn Sasse – for many sustained discussions on the 'border question'. The research unit is part of the Cluster of Excellence 'Contestations of the Liberal Script' (EXC 2055, Project-ID: 390715649), funded by the DFG under Germany's Excellence Strategy. The research unit also supported the translation of the book into English. Friederike Kuntz and Julian Heide provided me with astute comments and suggestions for improving the manuscript; Michael Zürn gave in-depth feedback, encouraging me to repeatedly sharpen and clarify my argument; Jan-Werner Müller, Sebastian Conrad and Tanja Börzel asked questions that challenged me to keep thinking. Katja Kerstiens closely checked and corrected the manuscript. It goes without saying that none of the people mentioned above is responsible for possible misinterpretations or incomplete lines of argument. The Mercator Stiftung supported me with a Mercator Senior Fellowship, without which I would have been unable to write this book. Many thanks go to Wolfgang Rohe, Michael Schwarz and the staff of the Stiftung. I would also like to thank my German publisher, C. H. Beck, for accepting the book in their Edition Mercator series. My editor, Matthias Hansl, took a keen interest in the book and provided excellent support and advice.

1

Borders Are Back!

The dramatic images from the Greek-Turkish border that flickered across our television screens in spring 2020 could hardly have packed a greater punch: buses carrying thousands of refugees across Turkey to the border, Turkish security forces herding people towards the border, wretched encampments with washing hung out to dry, Greek border police hectically putting up concrete barriers and rolling out barbed wire, stun grenades flaring and tall heavy-duty fans blowing clouds of tear gas over to the Turkish side of the border. Cut to John F. Kennedy Airport, New York, at almost exactly the same time. Hundreds of passengers stood for hours, crammed into narrow passageways, waiting to be allowed into the US. The requirements for entry into the US had been tightened overnight because of rising numbers of Covid-19 infections, resulting in chaotic scenes. Ad hoc orders to question incoming travellers and take their temperatures led to massive delays and bottlenecks, which the airport was not equipped to cope with. People were pushed together into tightly packed, slow-moving queues. Commentators spoke of a human petri dish, offering ideal conditions for the spread of the virus.

Both scenes are emblematic of the blocking and sorting effect of borders: borders stop people, push them back, lock them out, act as filters. Thanks to scenes like these, borders have made a dramatic return to our consciousness in recent years. After the fall of the Berlin Wall in November 1989, many people succumbed all too readily to the illusion that we were living in an age of opening barriers, expanding mobility and increasingly permeable borders. In 2009, 'border' – along with 'paternoster lift', 'cheese on sticks' and 'tape recorder' – even made it into the *Lexikon der verschwundenen Dinge* (Dictionary of Forgotten Things),[1] as if it were something that belonged in a museum. Berlin, as the city once divided by the Iron Curtain, is especially symbolic of the end of a world structured by closed borders. One of the demands made in autumn 1989 was that 'The Wall must go'; today, the border strip is nothing more than a tourist attraction.

At first glance there seems to be much to confirm this view of borders as a relic of the past. Trend data show that cross-border transactions and movements have risen enormously in the past three decades and even before that.[2] Borders are crossed more and more frequently, their compartmentalizing character seems to have softened and they are perceived as increasingly permeable. This applies not only to communication via the internet, trade and production chains, finance flows, and the dissemination of information and cultural goods, but also to the various forms of human mobility with which this book is concerned. More and more often, for an ever larger group of people, leaving the inner space of the nation-state is becoming an increasingly self-evident step; crossing and recrossing the border seems like the normal state of affairs. In analyses of these changes in the 1990s and 2000s, hypotheses about 'vanishing borders'[3] or the 'borderless world'[4] – all of them conjuring up obsolescent or increasingly porous borders – were not figments of the academic imagination, but often-evoked and much-quoted tags, which seemed to encapsulate major trends. Here, globalization was regarded as a powerful driving force, with a near irresistible capacity to open, or in some cases break down, borders.

In social theories from the same period, disembedding from place-bound contexts and the deterritorialization of social relations were even identified as crucial elements in the development of modernity.[5] The theory was that we were no longer shackled to a single place, but extended our social relations over great distances, constantly crossing borders and striding around the globe in our seven-league boots. A few decades earlier, a period spent abroad had still been viewed as an 'exotic' exception; now cross-border social, family, romantic and employment relationships and transnational CVs had become routine and normal.[6] Processes of deterritorialization, denationalization and transnationalization took centre stage; clinging to what was limited, national and immobile was seen as backward-looking, since it ignored the powerful dynamic opening up previously closed and contained societies. There was even talk of an 'atopian society', where territorial limitations were radically abolished; some saw the 'world society' appearing on the horizon.[7] It seemed that nothing stood in the way of global interaction – or at least nothing in which borders played a major role.

Although this view may not have been an optical illusion, it overemphasized the debordering character of globalization and produced a one-sided image. And while an increase in 'border traffic' is often taken as evidence that a border has become more permeable or has ceased to function, this is by no means an obvious conclusion. Perhaps the focus on the dissolution of borders is partly to do with the specific way that 'frequent travellers'[8] – the group responsible for the majority of border crossings – experience the world. For this group – i.e., those who are able and authorized to travel – globalization mostly means opening, debordering and greater opportunities for mobility. The most prominent proponents of the discourse of globalization are undoubtedly part of this highly mobile group, able to popularize their theses on podiums in Boston, Cape Town and Seoul. People who are allowed to travel themselves, and whose mobility is scarcely restricted by borders, may be inclined to generalize from their own experiences and to underestimate contrary developments. Perhaps this is a *déformation professionnelle* on the part of conference tourists? But then again, this is probably not the place for such speculations.

It would be wrong, of course, to suggest that experiences of border crossing are limited to a small number of privileged groups – on the contrary, they extend far beyond these groups and are global in scale. And yet the experience of crossing borders quickly, smoothly, comfortably and without hindrance is by no means a ubiquitous phenomenon. For a large part – the majority! – of the world's population, the everyday experience of borders is one of exclusion, denial of mobility, and obstruction; of being on the outside, of rebordering. It is still the case that borders are the place where, in the words of the pioneering sociologist Georg Simmel, the 'merciless separation of space' ('das unbarmherzige Auseinander des Raumes')[9] becomes most obvious. At borders, critical processes of social division take place.[10] Even in the global society, we live in parcels of territory, and borders take on functions of filtering, separation and circulation management. They are not just places where checks are undertaken: many groups are turned back at borders. The situation at the Greek-Turkish border, mentioned at the beginning of this chapter, is certainly not an isolated case.

So the idea that the process of globalization is essentially one of dissolution of borders is simplistic, and in my view misleading. Even under conditions of globalization – particularly under these conditions, in fact – border regimes enforce territorial control and selectivity; they are powerful 'sorting machines' of the globalized world. There is therefore no real scientific justification for associating or equating globalization with porous or disappearing borders, rather than seeing it as a complex, inherently contradictory process. This default setting has turned blind spots into a scientific programme and suppressed any contradictory developments. These developments can only be deciphered if we cease to consider globalization solely in terms of cross-border transactions or flows. Instead we need to take a much more comprehensive view, seeing it as a relatedness that extends beyond the nation-state and the national society.[11] Globalization is not just about crossing borders; it is about modes of interdependence that include the hardening of borders, the denial of mobility, and border selectivity. The question to ask about globalization is not just how 'old borders' are opening or disappearing, but how borders are changing, and what 'logic of sorting' is in operation at the 'new borders'. Under conditions of extensive, indeed massive flows of mobility, borders are designed to allow only the desired mobility, and to control and, if need be, prevent unwanted mobility. In such an understanding of globalization, opening and closing belong together; to grasp the dialectic core of globalization and give it sharper conceptual definition, we can even speak of a globalization of opening and a globalization of closing. These are two sides of the same coin.

It is a widespread misunderstanding to reduce the new forms of closing that are constitutive of globalization to mere (ideologically motivated) anti-globalization. In fact, the reverse is true: because globalization exists, borders become more important, are gradually upgraded, and are used as sorting machines. The closure and control of borders is therefore not only compatible with globalization, but an integral part of it and a prerequisite for opening. To re-emphasize this point: globalization does not cause borders to disappear, but induces and constantly enforces closing, selectivity and the intensification of control. Of course, insistence on border functions can also manifest itself as anti-globalization. In most cases, however, it is a facet of globalization itself, forms of closing in the service of globalization. In globalization, opening and closing go hand in hand. One indication of this is the unwillingness of those advocating closure to restrict their own mobility privileges and the benefits they derive from open borders.

The Covid crisis was a shock, especially for Western societies, catapulted from a situation of freedom of movement and high mobility to a state of stasis and interrupted mobility. When the dramatic images from Wuhan first reached us in January 2020, they were extremely disturbing: roadblocks; police officers taking aim with thermometers as if they were guns; people shut into their apartments, calling out words of encouragement to each other; soldiers patrolling the street; closed railway stations, bus stations and airports. Just a few weeks later, many civil liberties and fundamental rights that we had seen as unassailable were also restricted in the 'West'. No event since the Second World War has so dramatically altered the political geography, causing states in all continents to close their borders and access routes overnight. With the exception of a handful of countries, nearly all UN member states took measures to close their borders in order to stop the spread of the virus. These included entry bans, the construction of fences and barriers, border checks, the interruption of international air travel, visa restrictions, demands for health information, and quarantine rules. Within a short space of time, populations were territorially fixed and separated from each other. Overnight, the highly mobile global society became a society of inmates, locked into national compartments.

Such a dramatic, worldwide closure of borders is undoubtedly exceptional; this is why it strikes at the heart of our collective self-image. It brings to the surface something that remains concealed in normal conditions: the state as a specific ensemble of territoriality, authority and control, which can use its extensive rights of intervention to structure social relations and forms of movement, and which permits or prevents mobility and residence. This reveals the fact that the nation-state – despite all prophecies of doom – still has substantial powers to separate spaces and suppress mobility with its border policies. The state is not just a supernumerary of globalization, a weak, powerless actor that can only gaze passively at the phenomenon of border crossing. On the contrary: its power, often concealed and withheld, has emerged unmistakably in the pandemic. It has reinforced the element of territorial control in spectacular fashion, and made the most of its capacity to isolate itself and others. The political concept behind this policy of closure was one central to the notion of sovereignty – the idea of defence against external (and internal) dangers.

Now this close connection between the state and its borders does not only come into being when epidemics break out; it is actually always with us. So the Covid crisis does not roll back globalization; it reveals – perhaps surprisingly for some – its otherwise obscured and overlooked flip side. There is hardly any other area of politics where we find so many different and sometimes contradictory developments occurring simultaneously: opening and closing, the dissolution and reinforcement of borders, the easing and intensification of control, mobilization and immobilization. To precisely observe this ambiguous development, however, we need to move away from the conventional idea of the border as a physical barrier or boom gate. The border of globalization is not the same as that of the nation-state container, or of the twentieth-century territorial model of national societies. Today we face an ensemble of places, technologies and structures of control, which can facilitate, channel or prevent mobility. The checkpoint on the periphery of the territorial state, opening or closing the border for travellers, is an obsolescent model. The border of the twenty-first century is moving away from the borderline, and, in spatial terms, reaching far beyond the national container. Although the nation-state remains the point of reference, we can understand the border itself as part of globalization. To uncover this new politics of the border, we will look beyond the static borderline, the border hut, and the red-and-white-striped barrier, and ask: How does the border as a sorting machine operate today? How is border control changing, politically, spatially, and technologically? What forms does it assume, what functions does it perform?

As stated above, my perspective on the border centres on the mobility of persons (not goods, information, cultural artefacts, finance flows, etc.). It is not possible, however, and nor is it my intention, to consider all the functions relevant here; instead the focus is on the operative functions of control. Other functions, relating to identity, integration or symbolic demarcation or distinction, will be given a more cursory treatment, and border conflicts and secessionist movements will also not be discussed in detail. As I see it, borders represent processes, technologies and infrastructures, which are used to enforce sorting procedures and to regulate the interplay between territoriality, circulation and residence. Borders perform two kinds of sorting function: the first is spatial/territorial, and the second relates to mobility. The spatial function could be described as separation: borders separate territories and populations from one another. The mobility-related function can be described as selectivity: borders filter people. Both aspects, however, are closely interlinked. Historically, the spatial/territorial function – the 'where' of the border – has played a major role in the self-assertion of states. Over the course of history, borders have been disputed and borderlines have shifted; often the concept of the border or frontier has included the military enforcement and fortification of a borderline. Today, border practices and regimes are much more focused on the filtering and regulation of mobility: the border still performs a spatial/territorial organizing role, but the emphasis has shifted to the selectivity function. From the perspective of mobility, the border is responsible for marking and enforcing distinctions: between those who are allowed to pass and those who are stopped or turned back, between desirable and undesirable travellers. Today's borders are no longer really about states asserting themselves against rival neighbouring states, but more about the management of mobility, about border crossings.[12]

My aim in this book is to examine these reorganized borders, keeping my observational radar sharply attuned to their functions. My hypothesis is that, in terms of the movement of persons, we are certainly not heading towards a borderless and deterritorialized society. On the contrary, borders, border fortifications and border control are part of globalization. They are, however, undergoing a radical process of operative, technological and spatial change, in order to become performant borders that support globalization. As a starting point for further reflection, I want to begin by recapitulating the classic connection between territoriality and border control, because it is of crucial importance for our modern 'image of the border', with its fixation on the physical borderline (Chapter 2). I will then turn to the debordering imperative of the literature of globalization, and counter it with the idea of a globalization that simultaneously imposes and removes borders – a dialectic of debordering and rebordering (Chapter 3). Chapter 4 will not only show that globalization has coincided with a rising interest in fortification and with new wall-building activities around the globe; it will also deal with the factors behind the new drive to seal borders, and with the precarious camps forming at these borders, in which people are gathered together, forced into bottlenecks, stopped in their tracks. The next topic is the filtering function of the border: I argue that this was always inherent in borders, but has been adjusted with increasing precision in the wake of globalization, so it is now possible to speak of a 'global mobility divide' (Chapter 5). Chapter 6 focuses on 'smart borders', a recent development in the use of digital technologies of surveillance, authentication and classification, which are rendering traditional, paper-based forms of control obsolete. Another element of the change in border regimes is the emergence of new macroterritorial arrangements as part of projects of regional integration (Chapter 7). Here new areas of circulation are being created, above the nation-state but below the global level, generating openness in their internal relations but reproducing or even increasing closure in their external relations. The last topic to be considered is developments such as the extraterritorialization of control, the displacement of control, and the use of technologies of control, along with strategies of 'remote control' focused on transit countries or travellers' countries of origin (Chapter 8).

The book traces the transformation of the border into a sorting machine. This term is a metaphor intended to highlight the selectivity of border crossings and border control. My analysis is not focused on specific cases or historical epochs, but I will use examples and trends of change to substantiate my arguments. The panorama

– however presumptuous this may sound – is global. The idea is to show that the old model of national territorial sovereignty and control of personal mobility has been replaced by a new border arrangement that is replicated on various scales (as summarized in Chapter 9). This leads to a substantial differentiation and interweaving of the border policies with which states attempt to maintain territorial control and simultaneously facilitate and prevent mobility. The result is an intricate control system with different scales, which has long since lost its close connection to national territories. Today the border as a sorting machine is a complex arrangement that subjects mobility to a paradigm of security, operates via intricate spaces of control, produces zones of circulation, takes its orientation from the social figure of the trustworthy traveller, and generates a global hierarchy of unequal rights to mobility. The border of globalization is a border where inequality is created and perpetuated.

2

Statehood, Territoriality and Border Control

Anton Dendemarchenko advertises his services as a tour guide by promising to show visitors 'the country that does not exist'. This is Transnistria, at the south-eastern tip of Europe, not far from the Black Sea, but unfortunately without access to it. Visitors here are met with great curiosity. While the locals are thoroughly informed about world events from the internet and television, what they really want to know is why foreigners would stray into this little country. Anton, however, understands its appeal: where else could you take a journey in time into the 'Soviet century',[1] and encounter bombastic architecture with Soviet stars, tanks transformed into monuments, or old Volgas, Ladas and Zaporozhets by the roadside? Anton has turned this into a business model. And in some ways this tract of land really does seem to be in a state of stasis.

Wedged between the Republic of Moldova and Ukraine, the country that does not exist extends 200 kilometres from north to south and is roughly twenty kilometres wide. Half a million people live here: Moldovans, Russians and Ukrainians. When the Soviet Union disintegrated, Transnistria split off and made a push for independence – but without success. Today it is dependent on financial and military support from Russia, and has become the pawn of interest-driven regional politics. On the one hand, Moscow wants this unresolved territorial conflict to thwart any potential bid for EU membership by Moldova. On the other hand, it sees control of this small strip of land as a way to keep neighbouring Ukraine under its thumb. If the Republic of Moldova were to join the EU without Transnistria, the outer border of the EU would run directly through a region that was once administratively and culturally integrated, with severe consequences for local social networks, families and economic connections.

Transnistria is an enclave with well-controlled borders, and with little involvement in the global circulation of people, goods and capital. No member state of the United Nations recognizes Transnistria as an independent state; the only countries to do so are Abkhazia, Artsakh (formerly Nagorno-Karabakh) and South Ossetia – all of them territories with a similarly unresolved status in international law, and all of them bones of geopolitical contention. These territories and Russia are the only places where Transnistria has diplomatic posts. The joint embassy of Abkhazia, Artsakh and South Ossetia is found behind an office door on the first floor of a rather uninviting building. If you knock on the door, you will nearly always find it locked. The embassies do not appear to have much to do. Anton explains: 'Since we're not recognized, travelling with a passport from Transnistria isn't so easy.' So the inhabitants of this would-be state have to improvise, by obtaining a second passport from Moldova, Russia, Romania or Ukraine – a strategy largely tolerated by the government. Transnistria's relationship with its neighbours remains precarious, however. An urgent trip to see a doctor in the Moldovan capital, Chișinău, failed because Anton was turned away by the border guards. And for a time, only women and children were allowed to travel to nearby Odessa because Ukraine feared that men might join the pro-Russian militias in the eastern part of the country.

Transnistria offers us a very telling demonstration of how difficult and complex the interplay between state sovereignty, territoriality and mobility is. Without state authority, international recognition, a valid passport, consolidated territoriality and stable relations with neighbouring countries, the place of a political entity and its inhabitants in the international community of states remains uncertain and precarious. In our minds, the case of Transnistria seems like an oddity, a bizarre outlier (though not the only one), diverging from the normality of state sovereignty. The parcelling of the world's surface into territorial states, the topography of different countries, the associated state authority, and the passport that identifies individuals as citizens and grants them certain rights – today all these things seem so self-evident that we hardly question them.

Historically, however, this modern form of statehood is a very recent invention. It replaced the state based on personal bonds (*Personenverbandsstaat*), which was shaped by personal relations of dependence and loyalty, or other forms of patrimonial rule. Gradually, the patchwork of overlapping dominions and affiliations disappeared, a process often accompanied by violent conflicts, and the model we know today, the territorial state with fixed borders, took shape. The Peace of Westphalia in 1648 marked the emergence of a political order in which states – inwardly and outwardly sovereign, holding a monopoly on the use of force, marked by clear borders, and equal to one another in status – became the central actors in an international system. It must be noted that this was initially a European model, which did not apply either to the subjugation of other territories by the European colonial powers or to the forms of political rule in other regions of the world. In large parts of Europe, however, the old order of unclear territorial claims was replaced by an understanding that granted each state 'its' territory. The state thus became both the 'occupier' and the 'owner' of a portion of the earth's surface, thereby acquiring the power to decide what should happen in this area. The basic principle behind this possessive concept of territory was that where there is one state, there cannot be another one. This exclusivity refers to the surface area, but also to residence and personal mobility. A person cannot be in two states simultaneously; anyone who crosses a border enters another state.

In the classic theory developed by the Austrian scholar of constitutional law Georg Jellinek, the state is defined by three elements: territory, nation (i.e., a resident population), and state authority (i.e., a form of governance covering the territory).[2] The modern state represents a specific form of the territorialization of the political, an ensemble of territory, authority and rights that has evolved over history.[3] Here, territoriality is not just a land area; instead, it is defined as control over an area, creating a corresponding social, political and geographical space. According to an influential definition by the geographer Robert D. Sack, territoriality is not simply an expanse of territory, but a strategy to control people, relationships and things by controlling space.[4] Territoriality is always accompanied by processes of classification, categorization and licensing, by decisions about who is granted entry, who is allowed to reside where, and what transactions – beyond a defined territory – are permitted or not permitted. In principle, this understanding of territoriality can be scaled to any space, be it our own garden, a factory site, or a confederation of states. At present, however, the state still embodies the most influential and the most legally codified form of the territorial principle.

The reason why the territorial principle has always played such a major role in the organization of statehood is obvious: spatial-physical sorting is essentially the most efficient way imaginable to implement processes of social classification and achieve the associated aim of imposing control. This is why states, in their formative phase, made a tremendous effort to take 'possession' of their own territory and bring it under control – with the result that the term 'country' is now understood mainly in territorial-geographical terms. Territorially structured social orders can always be understood as border arrangements: borders serve to define countries' external boundaries, but also to homogenize societies internally – for example, by the nationalization of the economy, language policies, political unification, the development of identity and loyalty, or the control of agents of socialization (education system). At the same time, they serve to regulate border crossings, for example by their own citizens, migrants, tourists, the transport of goods, cultural artefacts, etc.[5] Processes of institutional 'assimilation' and the fixing of border-lines have had a profound impact on local conditions, especially in border regions marked by interaction with neighbours.[6]

With the rise of the modern nation-state in the nineteenth century, this model became more complex, developing its own ideas about the nation and the people, its own political and cultural symbols, and institutional arrangements for social integration. In his pioneering works, the Norwegian political scientist Stein Rokkan made the constructive suggestion that the process of nation-state formation should be understood from the perspective of two interconnected spaces, 'territorial space' and 'membership space', which both perform their own border-demarcating functions.[7] The territorial structure allows the spatial expansion of political power and sovereignty, while membership space is primarily – but not exclusively – defined by citizenship as an 'instrument of social closure'.[8] The dual nature of the state is revealed by the fact that it is both a territorial and a membership state. Many people are able to cross the border, but in general only those who have citizenship of the relevant state can claim full membership rights. The state can refuse entry to non-citizens, thus exercising 'external exclusion', but it can also practise 'internal exclusion' by distinguishing between citizens and non-citizens when granting access to rights and resources.[9] In the stationary 'society of inmates', a purely theoretical construct in which all citizens remain within 'their' territory, this latter distinction has little relevance. In the age of migration and of constant border crossings, however, it is increasingly politicized and challenged, since the legal and social exclusion of long-term or permanently resident non-citizens can hardly be legitimized.

As already emphasized, the above-described connection between state formation and territorial closure was, at first, a specifically European experience. We often tend to generalize from this, but we should be more cautious – even if the territorial model of state and society is now established throughout the world. On the African continent, for example, there were no endogenously driven processes of border formation; instead, the colonial powers drew the borders at the Berlin Conference of 1884/85 and divided the continent by countries – and among themselves. So the foundation for the territorial order of Africa, which is largely still in place today, was not created during the development of sovereign nation-states, but was the result of the jostling between distant colonial powers. The territorial arrangement was imposed from the outside, while local conditions – for example, cultural, religious or social matters – took a subordinate role. The geography prevailing at the time was not determined to any great extent by what we generally think of as 'countries'; more important were spatial zones or areas that could not be understood as clearly separated territories. This mismatch was a recipe for long-term instability.

Borders are always artificial and arbitrary. Ultimately this can be said of any border, but it is particularly obvious in the case of Africa. A substantial incongruence between ethnic-cultural, social and political-territorial borders entails high political costs, since the resulting secessionist movements and territorial conflicts are difficult to pacify. In Africa, the number of 'partitioned cultural areas' is particularly high – the border between Nigeria and Cameroon alone cuts through fourteen culturally connected areas, according to relevant censuses, while the border of Burkina Faso divides twenty-one such areas.[10] Those advocating border revision have therefore called for a radical redrawing of borders in Africa, while sceptics have pointed out that the existing borders can actually be traced back to precolonial and postcolonial population divisions, so they are not without historical precedent.[11] Often the normative power of the facts is evoked: it is argued that the national territorial model has become established in Africa, as elsewhere, and that there is a clear trend towards territorial consolidation and sociopolitical acceptance of borders.

After the independence of the African states, the borders in place at the time were formally confirmed by the most important political actors. They assumed that it would not be possible to find a satisfactory solution to the existing border conflicts in the short or medium term, and saw it as essential to avoid new tensions during the precarious transition to national independence. This is why, in 1963, the founding charter of the Organization of African Unity (OAU), a forerunner to the African Union, included a commitment to defending national sovereignty and territorial integrity. In the following year – accepting the risk of possible disputes – the organization also committed to respecting existing borders. The reasoning was that, after the codification of the status quo, it was necessary to get used to it gradually. This means that, despite comparatively weak political institutions, Africa has had largely stable territorial borders since the late nineteenth century, and there seems to be no prospect of a practicable alternative model of 'rational' borders.[12] It can therefore be argued that the frontiers once forcibly imposed as 'foreign borders' have now become recognized 'African borders'.[13]

Even beyond the African continent, borders show a remarkable stability once they have been drawn. The political scientist Boaz Atzili has referred to this persistence as 'border fixity', highlighting the consistency and apparent immovability of territorial borders since the Second World War.[14] In the phase before the nineteenth century and even up to the middle of the twentieth century, borders were constantly moving: territories were in flux, the outlines of states were continually being redrawn on the world map, entire political geographies were changing. Today, however, the reconfiguration of national territories or expansionist land seizures are the exception. This observation holds true if we consider all borders worldwide, even if we can readily list numerous examples of border shifts, most recently the Russian aggression against Ukraine and the illegal annexation of Crimea. Several current border conflicts are aftershocks from collapsed or dissolved multiethnic states such as Yugoslavia or the Soviet Union. There are also forms of incremental border shift, such as the barbed-wire border between Georgia and South Ossetia, secured by the Russian military, which can even run straight through a family's orchard. The documentary *I Didn't Cross the Border, the Border Crossed Me*, by Toma Chagelishvili, shows this very vividly with the example of the village of Churvaleti.

The international norm of 'border fixity' can be seen as a key reason why territorial conflicts between states have declined – fixed borders are even regarded as the solution to the problem of rivalry between states. Since border-related violations of norms can result in political ostracism or sanctions, the costs of any attempt to change borders in one's own favour are relatively high. States may wish for different borders, but they rarely pursue these interests aggressively. However, the pacifying effects of this border norm are mainly to be found in places with strong, capable states, for example in North and South America, East Asia and Europe. They are less apparent in places with weak or – as we often, not without problems, hear today – 'failed' states, such as in sub-Saharan Africa. But the relation of cause and effect can also be presented differently: because there are fixed borders and therefore minimal territorial threats, states remain weak and have little incentive to centralize and to build up administrative and policing capabilities.[15] Alternatively, however, it could also be argued that fixed borders are most likely to remain ineffective in places where comparatively weak states come under the influence of strong regional powers, which consistently obstruct their neighbours' agency and sovereignty.

These days, a fairly substantial proportion of border conflicts are transformed into legal disputes. The International Court of Justice regularly hears cases of countries articulating rival territorial claims, and seeking a legal resolution or ruling.[16] Often the legal route is only taken after direct confrontations; occasionally it succeeds in avoiding military conflict, but sometimes it only delays it. It is mainly the after-effects of decolonization, unclear borderlines and secessions that keep border disputes alive. The countries involved in the dispute present various arguments in support of 'their' border – for example, existing treaties, geographical features such as mountain ranges or rivers, or aspects of cultural affiliation such as religion, language and ethnicity. Many states argue that the territories used to belong to them – an argument that can be linked to the idea of property rights in Western societies. Such rights are also the basis for claims to restitution.[17] Lastly, international law relies on the principle of *uti possidetis*: that borders should be based on the real territorial situation of a state, regardless of how this situation came about. According to this principle, countries should be restricted to their 'inherited territories', since claims to further territories can lead to a cascade of additional, retroactive demands.

In our discussion of borders we have so far focused on territorial consolidation and control. Now, however, we come to a second aspect, which is at least of equal importance. Borders do not create island states, alone in the vast ocean, or isolated enclaves of territoriality, but relations and exchanges between neighbours. Historically, the question of *where* the border lay was fundamental to the relationship between states and territorial authorities, but today the foremost question is 'how'[18] – that is, how a border operates, whether it can be crossed (or not), what forms of mobility it allows (or does not allow), and how checks are carried out at the border. Jürgen Habermas describes borders as 'internally operated "floodgates", meant to regulate the currents so that only the desired influxes (or outflows) are permitted'.[19]

Historically, the formation of (Western) nation-states was accompanied by a development that John Torpey has described as the 'monopolization of the legitimate means of movement'.[20] In an analogy with Max Weber's description of how the state monopoly on the legitimate use of force became established, Torpey reconstructs how the barriers to mobility previously erected by different social, religious and political actors or entities, and the rights to residence that had been granted by the same agents, were gradually eliminated, while border and mobility controls were 'nationalized' and their focus shifted to the external borders. It was the associated enclosure, fixing and regulation of populations that gave states the capacity to act, for example with regard to tax collection or compulsory military service. In most countries it is possible to move about freely within the territory (subject to property rights), but anyone wishing to cross a state border must accept state controls. The state has become the only legitimate actor when it comes to allowing and restricting mobility, and controlling borders at the edge of a territory.[21]

Historical studies have pointed out that it was the massive expansion of world trade between 1870 and 1914 that accelerated this codification and regulation of mobility.[22] The (apparently) paradoxical aspect of this first wave of globalization is that state systems of border control were put in place at exactly the time when countries were becoming more integrated into the global economy, and when worker mobility was rising enormously (at the time, capital was still comparatively immobile). In contrast to local and stationary societies, in which people rarely travelled and generally only went short distances, the mobility of globalization was of a different quality and quantity: partly because of the new modes of transport, more people were travelling longer distances. They did so mainly for economic motives – since globalized capitalism brought new push-and-pull forces. This large-scale mobilization caused states to take an interest in recording and channelling people's movements, granting residence permits, and excluding people. Legislators also turned their attention to the admission of victims of persecution, developing early versions of the right to asylum.[23] At the same time, new technologies came into use: for example, the fingerprint, once deployed solely to identify criminals, was converted into an instrument used by states and administrations to register the mobile population.[24] Before and during this first phase of globalization, control regimes were also established in other, non-Western regions of the world, such as the Ottoman Empire or India: these regimes transformed borders from transitional zones into controlled lines, often targeting specific (ethnic) groups. Some countries introduced population registers, while others opted for more rigid entry controls. The creation of an international passport system in the late eighteenth and early nineteenth centuries was a major step towards comprehensive regulation of cross-border mobility.[25]

We should probably avoid idealizing the control practices of state actors here: in the past it was rare for states to impose complete control on the most remote corners of their territory and on all sections of their border, and even today this is often not achieved. At the same time, there have always been different experiences of the border. For example, Stefan Zweig, in his autobiographical work *Die Welt von Gestern (The World of Yesterday)*, describes a very open and travel-friendly world: 'We could live a more cosmopolitan life and the whole world stood open to us. We could travel without a passport and without a permit wherever we pleased. No one questioned us as to our beliefs, as to our origin, race, or religion.'[26] The global historian Sebastian Conrad rightly emphasizes the fact that Stefan Zweig was describing these times as a white, educated, European man, not as a Polish seasonal worker in East Prussia or a Russian migrant in the US: 'And their experience of globalization was quite a different one: immigration procedures, hygienic controls, fingerprints and passports, citizenship laws, and exclusion acts all contributed, from the late nineteenth century, to the entrenchment of national borders. Between 1890 and 1914, imagined lines in Europe were turned into national borders.'[27] Conrad argues that while globalization has always encouraged the global circulation of people, it also reinforces national borders, and represents an increase in selectivity and control.[28] This foreshadows a development that can also be observed in the second wave of globalization: globalization itself is a driver of bordering processes.

These days it is a self-evident element of the concept of sovereignty of modern nation-states that 'whoever wishes to cross the border can legitimately be checked. The border is the place of legitimate state control, even without suspicion – in other words, it is the place where the state is entitled to be equally suspicious of everyone.'[29] At the border, the state monopoly on the control of mobility[30] becomes particularly visible, since the state has considerable latitude for decision-making when it comes to territorial access for 'foreign' individuals. The state is not required to treat all those crossing the border equally, nor does it have to justify itself for refusing entry to certain people or groups. The 'right to entry' is only weakly codified in international law. There is no absolute right to entry or residence, except in cases of humanitarian migration (asylum-seekers and refugees), where the state acknowledges protection status on the basis of international agreements or constitutionally guaranteed rights, or in cases of family reunification.

And yet when it comes to the issue of borders there is a tendency to draw fundamental distinctions between liberal and authoritarian states. Many countries, such as the socialist states of the eastern bloc or North Korea, have even denied their citizens the right to leave, which contravenes the UN's Declaration of Human Rights. From a liberal perspective, 'freedom in space is manifested as the opportunity for movement',[31] but at the same time this is constrained by the need to form and consolidate political communities – which is not met simply by assembling people who happen to be present (or are just passing through). Liberal states aim to strike a balance between the right to collective self-determination (which includes the option of excluding others) and individual rights to self-determination, protection and freedom of movement. It is often assumed that liberal states, when considering these matters, will give more weight to civil liberties, rights to protection and human rights than other forms of government.[32] For example, the political scientist Malcolm Andersen writes:

> There is undoubtedly a connection between border controls and the nature of political regimes. To simplify: authoritarian, repressive regimes are threatened by open borders and cannot tolerate them. ... By contrast, liberal regimes, with a respect for human rights and based on a market economy, cannot impose an exclusive and rigorously enforced border control regime without compromising their basic purposes.[33]

There is even a strand of liberal normative theory that questions whether the existence of borders and restrictions on mobility can be justified at all.[34] Empirically, however, it is highly doubtful whether liberal states can generally be assumed to be more open towards mobility and to have more liberal border regimes – regimes that also respect the principles of the rule of law. As I proceed, it will become clear that even liberal states – especially liberal states, in fact – reinforce the sorting function of borders, not least because they are looking for ways to circumvent their self-imposed liberal commitments and to expand their scope to prevent unwanted mobility.

In the following chapters I will focus on border control regulating the movement of persons. For me the crucial question is how cross-border personal mobility is regulated and channelled by states, and what forms of control it is subject to. In the first phase of globalization, people (as workers) were more mobile than capital, but now it seems that personal mobility is declining in relation to other forms of mobility. There is very little to suggest that states will ever show the same degree of openness towards people as they do towards finance and commodity flows; most states are wary of outsiders and at great pains to manage (i.e., to control and limit) access to their own territory. Before taking a detailed look at more recent developments in border control practices, I will turn, in the next chapter, to the megatrend of globalization. This is commonly, and to my mind erroneously, understood solely as a dissolution of borders. I will present the contrary argument that globalization is primarily a process of division: it grants mobility to some, but denies it to others, and it uses the border to sort the different groups. The globalization of opening and the globalization of closure are, in my view, two sides of the same coin. So how does this 'sorting machine' – the border – operate in the twenty-first century?

3

Opening and Closing:
The Dialectic of Globalization

'As far as I know it takes effect ... immediately.' This sentence – spoken by Günter Schabowski, a member of the East German Communist Party politburo, and quoted to death ever since – triggered the fall of the Berlin Wall. It was the answer to a question from a journalist at a press conference on 9 November 1989, about when the new rules for travel to Western countries would come into force. This ingenuous utterance was the starting signal for an unprecedented surge of East German citizens towards the border to West Berlin, which was eventually opened that same night by the security forces. But it was also a milestone in radical processes of change which put an end to the bipolar world of the East–West conflict. For people of my generation – or to be more precise, people from the same origins as me – the ninth of November is the date when we gained unimagined new freedoms, including the freedom of movement and the freedom to travel. Up till then, East German citizens had only been able to leave the country or travel to the West with extreme difficulty, and many had paid for the 'escape to freedom' with their lives. The political harassment ended overnight: a state that had kept its population locked in became what might be referred to emotively as an 'open society'. Ultimately, the concept of freedom is linked in the most elementary way with the right to move and not to be confined to one place.

Undoubtedly, the fall of the Berlin Wall has a special significance in the collective memory of Europe, and particularly Germany. Just as important for the opening of state-organized societies on both sides of the Iron Curtain, however, was the long-term social, political and economic transformation associated with 'globalization'. One definition of the term that is influential in the social sciences describes it as a process of change in the spatial organization of society, leading to an increase in the extent, intensity, speed and effect of cross-border transactions, circulation and communication.[1] In this interpretation, 'globalization' is a term denoting intensification: unlike the concept of globality, for example, it focuses on the ever-increasing circulation of goods, capital, people, etc. across national borders. In the majority of research on globalization, it is equated – or at least primarily associated – with debordering, i.e., with the elimination, dissolution or crossing of borders. The weakening and increasing porosity of borders are regarded both as the modus operandi of globalization and as its inevitable consequence – a view connected to the sweeping assumption that globalization is robbing borders of their interrupting function. If we do not reduce globalization to economic processes, but instead understand it as giving greater freedom to every individual, then the political appeal (and longstanding dominance) of this narrative of debordering is obvious. It is in the nature of borders, whether metaphorical or physical, that they limit the opportunities available to the individual. They constrain and exclude, and are therefore generally experienced as a loss or a restriction by those who encounter them. At the same time, borders can become an individual and collective resource, since they play a part in the constitution of affiliations and identities.

This aspect, however, has been largely disregarded in the euphoric discourse of globalization.

Sociology has tried to respond to the changes linked with globalization by abandoning the idea of a unified, clearly delimited and territorially fixed society – the 'society of inmates' confined to 'container states' – and turning to more dynamic and complex concepts of social order, networking and scaling. Severe and well-founded criticisms have been levelled at 'methodological nationalism',[2] arguing that societies can be understood less and less in terms of spatial separation and exclusivity, and can now only be viewed in their interconnectedness. Anthony Giddens, for example, has defined globalization as the intensification of worldwide relationships, leading to connections between distant places.[3] And yet this is not a completely new development. Even long before the latest wave of globalization there was mobility of capital, an internationally asymmetrical division of labour, and colonial relations of dominance and exploitation, none of which appeared in the image of the territorially bound and sovereign nation-state. Studies on transnationalization, the network society or the world society have explored these issues and developed new perspectives.[4] The postcolonial perspective also offers important insights into global and hierarchic interconnections.[5] From a position focusing more on 'globalization from below', the British sociologist John Urry has established a new 'paradigm of mobility', drawing attention to the movement of 'things' and people and thereby moving away from a stationary concept of society. Urry argues that the study of global flows, networks and diverse forms of movement produces a more realistic reflection of social conditions than social science surveys based on the assumption of fixed locations and relationships.[6]

Often, however, research on globalization is not about global entanglements, postcolonial relations of dominance, or the formation of transnational social spaces, but primarily about cross-border transactions and mobility, which readily lend themselves to empirical measurement. This approach focuses on cross-border movements and networks; its advantage is that a broad range of indicators of globalization can be generated. The KOF Globalization Index, an important source for globalization research, developed by ETH Zurich,[7] shows a massive rise in different forms of border crossing in key areas of society.[8] These forms include economic globalization (as measured, for example, by the international goods trade, cross-border services, the level of customs duties, and by direct investments or international bank transfers), social globalization (as measured by international telephone communication, tourist travel, the proportion of people from migrant backgrounds or the development of the freedom to travel), cultural globalization (as measured by the exchange of cultural goods or the number of McDonald's restaurants per head of population) and, finally, political globalization (as measured, for example, by the total number of foreign embassies in a country, the number of NGOs or the number of international treaties). We might argue about some of these indicators of globalization, and about whether the basic indicators constitute a more or less complete set. What is indisputable, however, is that massive increases can be shown across the whole spectrum (of these and other indicators), mainly between 1990 and 2010. After this the pace slows slightly and there are signs of saturation. The latest developments caused by the Covid pandemic show a decline, but this is probably only temporary – though some people are already predicting a phase of deglobalization.[9]

Cross-border human mobility matches the general trend: here too, there has been a striking increase, apparently confirming the prevailing emphasis on movement in globalization studies. Crossing borders – on foot, by road or rail, or by plane – has become routine, a mass phenomenon unknown to the generations before us. Air traffic alone (though recently brought to a standstill by the pandemic) shows huge rates of growth: from 1970 to 2019 the number of international air passengers increased more than tenfold, reaching more than 4.5 billion passengers per year. According to the United Nations World Tourism Organization (UNWTO), there were 25 million international tourist trips in 1950, and sixty times more – 1.5 billion – in 2019. On the level of individual experience, we do not need forensic tools to demonstrate how horizons of action and forms of movement have expanded beyond national 'containers'. In the 1950s, a study by the Allensbach Institute reported that only 26 per cent of respondents in a representative survey in Germany had ever experienced other countries by travelling or working abroad. For many of those who said that they had been in other countries, this was linked to wartime events.[10] Five decades later, in our own survey, nearly 60 per cent of the population stated that they had been abroad just in the previous twelve months.[11] The massive proliferation of overseas experiences, incessant border crossings, tourism, educational mobility and various forms of short- and long-term mobility can be interpreted as an 'increasing emancipation from space',[12] which is loosening ties to the nation-state.

Usually this data is taken as direct evidence of a decline in the structuring power of borders. It is argued that their barrier effect has been gradually eroded, perhaps even eliminated in many places. This argument is represented by economics-inspired notions such as 'the world is flat'[13] or 'world without walls',[14] highlighting the border-opening character of globalization. The popular hypothesis of a loss of control[15] has suggested that globalization is putting increasing pressure on the central attributes of statehood, such as sovereignty, territorial exclusivity and citizenship. Above all, the ease with which global finance flows or information can cross borders is taken as an indication that the state is barely able to maintain its old role of gatekeeper, and is losing its authority to close borders. Jürgen Habermas's description of the 'postnational constellation' echoes this idea that globalization is weakening the state: globalization 'conjures up images of overflowing rivers, washing away all the frontier checkpoints and controls, and ultimately the bulwark of the nation itself'.[16]

Similar arguments have been put forward with regard to migration and mobility: that the exclusionary power of state authority has been critically weakened, and that, despite restrictive immigration regulations, rigorous forms of closure can no longer be enforced.[17] It is argued that states, attempting to restrict migration with rigid immigration policies, border fortifications and territorial control, are condemned to failure, since these efforts are continually undermined by market forces, irregular migration, transnational networks and self-imposed humanitarian commitments. Even if the state wanted to stop migration, the argument goes, it is ultimately 'unstoppable', and borders are 'beyond control'.[18] The opening of borders is seen as inevitable, because (so the argument continues) globalization cannot be restricted to some sectors only; it will automatically spill over to different social spheres, including the mobility of people. If the economy is globalized, more cross-border mobility of persons will follow. The transnational circulation of goods, capital and information is thought to have border-eroding effects, 'they ... tear the borders they cross',[19] leaving openings for the movement of people. In keeping with this assumption of state powerlessness, even walls, the concrete manifestation of efforts to seal borders, are dismissed as symbolic political gestures. They are seen as merely simulating rather than actually embodying the state's capacity and authority to effectively control migration – as monuments revealing the decline of state sovereignty rather than its strength.[20]

It is clear even from these brief remarks that a close connection is often made between globalization and borders. I referred to this earlier as a narrative of debordering – though it must be added that this narrative is seldom explicitly stated. At the risk of a certain one-sidedness, but with the aim of presenting a more well-rounded argument, it may be observed that the concept of globalization has so far focused more on the overcoming and suppression of borders than on their adaptation or reinforcement.[21] There is a definite bias towards debordering; the crucial aspect of this worldview is the principle of movement and the opening of the 'container' of national society. This narrative includes three assumptions: first, that globalization is a worldwide process; second, that it is an inclusive process, which essentially encourages everyone to cross borders constantly; and third, that it brings spill-over effects from one area into adjacent areas (for example, economic integration is assumed to lead to more opportunities for mobility).

And yet a brief glance at the topic of global human mobility shows that travelling is a highly stratified area of activity. In international air travel, on the one hand, expanding route networks, falling fares and the easing of entry formalities have led to a massive rise in tourism and frequent talk of a 'world in movement'. On the other hand, the regions that have benefited disproportionately from this are those that could already have been regarded as highly mobile. It is mainly people from the Global North who travel, often within the OECD world, but also to the Global South. There is, in contrast, no sign of an extensive mobility network between countries of the Global South.[22] It is only since the early 2010s that we have been able to observe an increase in tourism in and out of Southeast Asia: here it is mainly rising incomes in China and India and the growth of a 'global middle class' that have boosted tourist activities.[23] But even in China only 10 per cent of the population travels internationally at present, probably the same proportion as in Europe in the 1950s. Europe, which constitutes only 10 per cent of the world's population, is responsible for more than half of all tourist trips worldwide, while Africa, with 17 per cent of the world's population, accounts for only 3 per cent of tourist travel.[24] The discrepancy is even more striking when it comes to air travel: it is estimated that only 3 per cent of the world's population flies at all in any given year, while 80–90 per cent of the world's human inhabitants have probably never set foot inside a plane in their lives.[25] Such distribution figures are an important indication of the unequal participation in processes of opening and mobility. They raise doubts about whether the globalization of opening should really be understood as a universal trend. At least for the mobility of persons, this assumption seems problematic. We have an abundance of examples of the physical and material hardening of borders; we are familiar with the various defensive measures against refugees and irregular migration; and we know about the intensification of controls – i.e., those developments that we associate with phrases such as 'fortress Europe', the 'wall around the West'[26] or a 'frenzy of nation-state wall building'.[27] At the same time, we can observe various developments that serve to intensify the barrier effect and selectivity of borders, such as the securitization of mobility, the displacement of border control and the 'smartification' of borders. The border of the twenty-first century, however, does not merely take the form of the traditional 'container state' border, organized along

its borderlines, but that of diverse, spatially fluid, organizationally diffuse and technologically altered forms of control, which channel or suppress personal mobility.

So is globalization really sufficiently understood if it is associated with debordering and porous borders, and not with closing, control and fortification? It would be more appropriate to speak of a divided globalization,[28] or to see globalization as a restratification, within which positions, resources, rights and opportunities are distributed in new ways – and according to global hierarchies. This view of globalization emphasizes its fragmentary nature, the structural asymmetries that come with it, despite various economic gains, and the fact that not everyone is included in it – let alone on an equal footing. This is an observation that is already well established in migration studies,[29] and which can be expanded to the field of mobility and borders,[30] where globalization has brought to the fore questions of exclusion and the prevention of mobility. Zygmunt Bauman, for example, emphasized the unprecedented polarizing effect of globalization on mobility: some groups can effortlessly overcome the limitations of space, while others are 'localized'.[31] He sees these processes as two sides of the same coin, and refers to this as 'glocalization'. Since globalization produces new rivalries, there are also 'losers', and people who are disadvantaged, marginalized or excluded. Large segments of the world population, in any case, do not enjoy the benefits of opening borders and reduced controls.

My point of departure is that there are, parallel to the debordering aspect of globalization, unmistakable trends of closure, border selectivity and control. If we do not reduce globalization to border crossing, but understand it more broadly, following Anthony Giddens's early definition, as an intensification of worldwide social relations,[32] this allows us to focus on bordering as well as debordering. In any case, the intensification of global connectivity is not manifested solely as a weakening of borders, but also as a change in their mode of operation. Borders are, after all, points of intersection that regulate exchanges, so it would be a gross simplification to see only the dismantling and opening of borders as an indicator of globalization, but not the complex process of transformation and adaptation of the border itself. Together with others, I understand globalization as an inherently ambiguous process, in which opening and closing occur simultaneously, because this is the way adjustments to external relations are made. According to this understanding, bordering and debordering are linked with and co-constitutive of globalization. We could even argue dialectically that border opening and border closure are causally connected.

The new walls built by states seeking to protect themselves against transnational terrorism or irregular migration can be just as much a reflection of globalization as a tourist flying to New York for a weekend's shopping, or China's investment in the New Silk Road. Alongside the globalization of opening, there is a globalization of closure, which is an inherent part of a world of cross-border movements and flows.[33] While some people are able to vastly expand their scope for mobility and cross borders with ever greater ease, others have exactly the opposite experience: closing and hardening borders, territorial exclusion and intensified control. Without the interventions that immobilize parts of the world's population and exclude them from the benefits of globalization, it would scarcely be possible to reduce or remove borders for the others.

This initial hypothesis implies that borders continue to fulfil their function and cannot be generally described as more porous. Their selective function, however, has changed under the conditions of globalization. Borders are arming themselves with new tools and systems to combine the benefits of opening – integration into a world market, opportunities for movement for their own citizens, tourism, etc. – with the desire for closure, motivated by a concern for security and fear of uncontrolled immigration. Borders must simultaneously be able to enact liberalization and control, freedom of movement and restrictiveness. They must operate as 'sorting machines', distinguishing between 'good' and 'bad', or rather between 'desirable' and 'undesirable' forms of mobility. This is not a completely new function, but globalization creates additional challenges, because the constant comings and goings across the border have increased so much that the old forms of control are no longer effective. An old-fashioned physical border, complete with roadblocks and boom barriers, would severely inhibit globalization, since it would disconnect countries – to their own detriment – from global processes.

In the chapters that follow, I will explore how the simultaneity of opening and closing has led to ever more complex control arrangements. What has often appeared to us as a dismantling or dissolution of borders is usually a metamorphosis of these borders. We could almost formulate a 'conservation law of borders' – a deliberate exaggeration to highlight this point. Most of the border barriers that have disappeared are reappearing in different forms. Showing a surprising adaptability, they stubbornly resist the perspective of a globalization of opening. Borders are also proving, in the age of globalization, to be key sites of exclusion, territorial control and the containment of mobility. Yet they are changing their form, place and methods. They are not relics of the past, but will probably continue to serve as the sorting machines of human mobility, even in the future. And how do they do this? How are they changing? I would like to answer these questions in the following chapters.

4

Fortification: Border Walls as Bulwarks of Globalization

At the Attari–Wagah border between India and Pakistan, a strange spectacle can be observed at five o'clock every evening: a border-closing ceremony celebrated by thousands of spectators. Indian and Pakistani soldiers in full dress uniform, adorned with peacock-like headdresses, march across the square, which is bisected by the borderline. On both sides, crowds assembled on semi-circular grandstands are whipped into a frenzy of enthusiasm – though the Indian side has a clear advantage in both numbers and noise level. People wave flags, the crowd bellows 'Long live India', women dance to pop music. The soldiers goose-step in parallel to the borderline, then two of them peel off and march towards the line. The flags of both countries are lowered, the soldiers call out a slogan across the border, slam the gate shut, throw it open again and finally close it emphatically. After three-quarters of an hour, the ceremony is over, and the border does not reopen until eight o'clock the next morning.

This daily ritual has been performed since 1959. The ceremony continued even when the two countries were embroiled in military conflict. Attari-Wagah is currently the only regular border crossing between the two countries; Pakistan and India are otherwise separated by a barbed-wire fence, around three metres high and 550 kilometres long. The border is partially electrified and is equipped with motion sensors and infrared cameras. Over time, mines have been laid in many places, making any attempt to cross the border potentially fatal. It was in 1947 that a political decision by the ruling colonial power led to the partitioning of the former British colony of India into what is now India and Pakistan. Since then an explosive conflict has simmered between the two countries, and the mutual sealing of their borders has become an act of political self-assertion. Despite the colourful ritual, the India–Pakistan border is the epitome of the fortified border, a border that serves as a barrier and is intended to prevent unregulated border crossings or 'border violations'. At such borders, isolation and separation are ostentatiously enacted with walls, fences, barbed wire, technical surveillance, strict control procedures and heavily armed personnel.

Given its structural qualities, the fortified border resembles the front line of a military conflict, though its aim these days is often to prevent 'irregular' border crossings. In the 1980s, this type of border was still part of the iconography of the East–West confrontation. But the role of borders as dividing lines between systems disappeared literally overnight; only the fortified border between North and South Korea survived the 'death' of this type of border. Only about a dozen fortified borders – that is, permanent structures, usually reinforced and cast in concrete – survived the historical caesura of 1989 and the years that followed, leading some people to believe that the age of wall-building and isolation was over. During the campaign for the European elections in 2014, the Pirate Party tried to capture the spirit of the times with posters proclaiming 'Borders are so 80s'. Yet this slogan, plastered all over Germany's pedestrian zones, was out of step with reality: at the time, walls and fences were becoming increasingly popular.

Since the turn of the millennium, we have been able to observe an inflationary revival of walled or fortified borders.[1] In the 1950s only two borders falling into the high-security category were built. The number then rose steadily into the 1980s, before dropping slightly after the collapse of the Soviet Union. Since the turn of the millennium, however, more fortified borders have been erected than in the five preceding decades – the curve is heading steeply upwards (see Figure 1).[2] Admittedly, the method of counting in the different studies varies, since there is no standard definition of a walled border. Nor is it always the case that the whole borderline between two territories is secured by a physical wall (see, for example, the US–Mexican border). Élisabeth

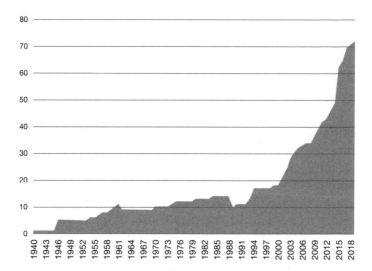

Figure 1: The rise in fortified borders (number)

Source: Élisabeth Vallet, 'State of Border Walls in a Globalized World', in Andréanne Bisonette and Élisabeth Vallet (eds.), *Borders and Border Walls: In-Security, Symbolism, Vulnerabilities* (London: Routledge, 2021), pp. 7–24. (Figure created by Élisabeth Vallet, Mathilde Bourgeon, Thalia D'Aragon-Giguère, Sofia Ababou, Frédérique Verreault.)

Vallet, a geographer at the University of Quebec at Montreal, estimates that there were twelve border walls existing in November 1989, and seventy-two in 2018.[3] Another study speaks of at least forty-five border walls and fifty-six secure border fences worldwide, though the border fortifications erected during the 'European refugee crisis' were not yet included in this number.[4] One thing is certain, however: walls are in fashion.

So the building of fences and walls is not declining in the globalized world society, but is increasing exponentially, just like cross-border transactions. This can be read as an indication that opening and interdependence may be accompanied by new efforts of separation and control. This would mean that our 'rendezvous with globalization' (as German politician Wolfgang Schäuble described it) was not just the result of worldwide migration, but also of global wall-building. Of course, this development is not taking us back to a world of drawbridges and hill forts. Unlike their historical predecessors, the new border walls are not characterized solely by their physical presence in space. The crucial fact is that they are the focal point of an ultra-modern, militarized arsenal of security systems and equipment.[5] The new walls have been armed with a multitude of new technologies, and 'digital border solutions' are springing up around them, generally supplied by Western companies (such as Magal Security Systems in Israel, Airbus in Europe or Securiport in the US). National wall-building has become a global business, and walled borders a successful and very lucrative Western export. They are also extremely dangerous: within just one decade, tens of thousands of people have been killed while trying to approach or cross a border.[6]

In the project 'The Borders of the World', my colleagues and I conducted our own survey of border infrastructures on a global scale.[7] In contrast to those researchers who focus on counting walls, our aim was to carry out a detailed survey of the physical-structural shape of land borders. What border infrastructures exist worldwide, and how are they distributed? Excluding small states and dependent or non-recognized territories, the total number of all land borders worldwide is 315; if we account for their dyadic character, there are 630 borders. For all these borders, we gathered dossiers of information, conducted online research, compiled photos and requested satellite images of border crossings via the Google Maps API. This information was aggregated and consolidated, enabling us to construct a five-level indicator of border infrastructure and produce a global map of these different infrastructures. The weakest border is what we call the 'no-man's land' border. Generally found in inaccessible and sparsely populated areas, this is left in its 'natural' state by the authorities, either because it is politically unimportant or because the state simply does not have the capacity to enforce comprehensive border controls. In contrast, 'boundary stone' borders are marked, but have generally been actively dismantled as part of regional integration processes. The Schengen area is the best-known example of this deinstitutionalization of borders and of the dismantling of border control facilities. The next step is the checkpoint border. Here the business of the border is focused on the border crossings, where roads widen, often into multiple lanes, as they approach the control posts. Traffic is directed towards the crossing points, where documents are checked. A fourth type is barrier borders, where the crossing points are flanked by physical obstacles such as fences or trenches, though these are not necessarily spread across the whole borderline. Finally, there are the fortified borders discussed above, reinforced with walls, fences, embankments and barbed wire. In general, these cover the whole borderline (or as much of it as is morphologically accessible) and are intended to prevent border crossings outside the official places of entry.

If we apply this classification to the total number of land borders worldwide (see Figure 2), then around 8 per cent of all borders can be classed as no-man's land borders. Around 12 per cent (seventy-seven in total) are boundary stone borders, where controls are absent or very low level and scarcely interrupt mobility. These can essentially be characterized as open borders. The classic checkpoint border can be found on nearly 60 per cent of the borders we looked at. One-fifth of borders – 130 in total – can be classified as either barrier borders

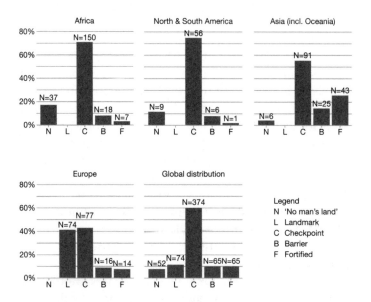

Figure 2: Distribution of different border infrastructures across continents (in percentages)

Source: Border infrastructure data: Steffen Mau, Fabian Gülzau and Kristina Korte, 'Grenzen erkunden: Grenzinfrastrukturen und die Rolle fortifizierter Grenzen im globalen Kontext', in Martina Löw, Volkan Sayman, Jona Schwerer and Hannah Wolf (eds.), *Am Ende der Globalisierung: Über die Re-Figuration von Räumen* (Bielefeld: transcript, 2021), pp. 129–152.

or fortified borders (sixty-five of each type). Élisabeth Vallet gives a similar figure for hardened borders as a proportion of all border dyads.[8] Her data also shows that this type of border consistently made up less than 5 per cent of all borders from the 1980s to the early 1990s, and that this figure only rose to 20 per cent after that. The fortified borders include the 'demilitarized zone' between North and South Korea and the border between the US and Mexico (referred to by some Americans as the 'Tortilla Wall'). But they also include the less famous borders between Algeria and Morocco and between Saudi Arabia and Yemen, the walls around South Africa, and the borders between Turkmenistan and Uzbekistan, between Botswana and Zimbabwe, and between Saudi Arabia and Oman. Since 2015, Turkey has been busy building walls: nearly two-thirds of the roughly 900-kilometre border between Turkey and Syria is reinforced by a wall, complete with barbed wire, concrete blocks and watchtowers, and now a 'security wall' is also being built on the border to Iran.

Fortified borders are a global phenomenon, but they are not appearing everywhere, and certainly not to the same extent. Interestingly, they are particularly common in Asia: on this continent, 40 per cent of all land borders show features of fortification, or are at least barrier borders. In Europe, 16 per cent of all borders are – still – fortified, while in Africa and North and South America one in ten borders falls into this category. At the same time, walled borders are often to be found at the points where the Global North meets the Global South – that is, in places where very unequal living conditions and levels of prosperity are juxtaposed. The borders of Melilla and Ceuta, the Spanish enclaves in North Africa, are secured by two fences, several metres high, with a control strip between them that is accessible to vehicles and monitored by video cameras. A brief glance at this barrier should make it clear that, if it were not for the Mediterranean, the southern border of Europe would not look very different from the (rightly) criticized border between the US and Mexico. It also makes it plain that there is no straightforward affinity between a political or economic system and the type of border design: walled borders are found in authoritarian and democratic states, in stable and failed states, in the Global North and the Global South, and in rich and poor countries.

How is it possible that, in a world of perpetual border crossings, mass tourism, digitization and the 'global emporium', walls are regaining importance and seemingly reimposing the old order? The increasing militarization and enforcement of border installations can perhaps be interpreted as a 'countermovement to the degree of opening that has already occurred, and [a reflection of] the need for renewed closure, based on the wish to protect the self against the incursion of the other'.[9] But it is also possible to see these efforts to seal borders as an essential component of globalization itself. Even in globalization, the state overtly uses territorial means to assert its influence, and to prevent globalization from becoming an 'uncontrolled flow' with unwanted side-effects. This would mean that the simultaneous occurrence of fortification and border crossing is not a coincidence, but the result of a dialectic of opening and closing. We could even say that the two things spring from the same origin.

Walls are always viewed as a code for the isolation of territories, perhaps even for the sealing of their borders. And yet there are very few border walls that are impermeable. This applies even to very closed-off territories: even on the border between North and South Korea, which is regarded as impregnable, there are visitor centres. The border between Morocco and Algeria has been considered to be completely closed since a bomb attack in Marrakesh in 1994, yet daring individuals wanting to visit friends on the other side use their own ladders to climb over it, and smuggling is an everyday affair. At the time of the Berlin Wall, the central departure hall for travel from East to West Berlin was known as the Tränenpalast ('Palace of Tears') for the many scenes of farewell that took place there. And even the conflicted border between India and Pakistan has recently shown an interesting form of permeability: on 9 November 2019 (ironically on the thirtieth anniversary of the opening of the Berlin Wall), a border corridor was created – based on an agreement between the two states – allowing Indians to visit a shrine in Pakistan, four kilometres from the border. A section of motorway and a passenger terminal were built especially, facilitating rapid processing of up to 5,000 travellers per day. Visitors can stay for the day and do not need a visa. The whole zone is controlled and guarded.

The walled border cements the separating function of the border, but is not limited to this function. Most border walls have checkpoints and allow cross-border traffic. Most are crossed daily by thousands, sometimes tens of thousands, of commuters and tourists, some are even among the busiest borders in the world. The walled border embodies a draconian architecture of closure, but it is usually not targeted at everyone, only at certain groups, whose mobility it seeks to contain. In the majority of cases, then, the new walls and fences are not warfare borders or frontiers, built as protection against an enemy, but sorting machines, designed to distinguish effectively between desirable and undesirable border crossings. This is 'modulated mobility by fortification',[10] that is, a specific combination of fortification and mobility, passable to varying degrees. This means that even the fortified border is generally at least partially permeable. Sometimes – for example in the case of the fence between Hungary and

Serbia, built as a reaction to the uncontrolled entry of refugees – the border does not make much difference to the cross-border mobility of immediate neighbours, but blocks the way for other groups. The majority of states maintain walls or fortifications as filtering borders, so they can reap the benefits of cross-border interchange. Only a minority, mainly autocratic states with an isolationist self-image, aim to achieve complete closure with these borders. So it is not the physical wall itself that makes the difference, but its operative function.

The specific reasons for the construction of walls and separation barriers are varied. Obviously not all of these borders are, strictly speaking, 'walls of globalization'. Some walls have outlived the purpose for which they were initially built and have simply remained standing. The Great Wall of China in its current form goes back to the Ming Dynasty, and was built to protect China against tribes of Mongolian horsemen from the north – who are unlikely to pose any threat to the People's Republic in the present day. A certain proportion of fortified borders have their origins in frozen conflicts: during the 'Cold War', the border between Eastern and Western Europe separated two highly armed rival systems locked in a mutual state of siege. In other cases, border fortifications are intended to emphasize territorial claims, as in the Kashmir conflict between India and Pakistan. Another example is the 'Green Line' running through Cyprus, which is secured by walls in some places and barbed wire in others. A third example is the 'Berm' in the western Sahara, a sand embankment built up by the Moroccan state, reinforced with mines and trenches. The 'War on Terror' has triggered a number of more recent border projects, aimed at preventing attacks by terrorists – whose operations usually cross national borders.[11] In this case, the fortified border is understood as an 'anti-terrorist structure': examples are the separation barrier at the border between Israel and the West Bank, and the barrier between Saudi Arabia and Yemen, intended as a defence against Al-Qaeda terrorists.

In parts of the literature, the acronym CTA (clandestine transnational actors) is used to group together the different forms of unwanted border crossing to which the new walls, embankments and fences are meant to respond.[12] This is an imprecise term, which mixes such diverse phenomena as transnational terrorism, cross-border human trafficking, drug smuggling, and illegal border crossings by people in poverty and need. More than 90 per cent of officially stated reasons for the construction of border walls are divided between security issues (29 per cent), immigration (42 per cent) and 'smuggling' (20 per cent).[13] These vague motives encapsulate the perspective of a state which hopes that its own border policies will prevent all border crossings perceived as undesirable or threatening. The actual effect of enhanced and reinforced border structures is controversial. Janet Napolitano, secretary of homeland security in the Obama administration, once said: 'Show me a 50-foot wall, and I'll show you a 51-foot ladder.'[14] It is sometimes argued that walls hardly reduce the number of irregular migrants, since these people usually enter legally and then simply stay on once their visa has expired. In general, it is difficult to judge the efficacy of fortified borders because wall-building is usually part of a package of other measures involving the military, the border police and migration policy, so it is not clear what exactly is responsible for the effects.[15] Recent research has at least given some indication that the existence of walls and fences could potentially deter or reduce cross-border terrorist events.[16]

What determines whether or not a wall is built on a border? In our own research we have chosen a hypothesis of homophily as the starting point for investigating border infrastructures (here the border is always viewed as a dyad between two neighbouring states).[17] This hypothesis posits that the hardness of the physical border decreases as the similarity between neighbouring countries increases, and, conversely, that borders become harder as the discrepancies between countries grow. In other words, substantial differences in political, cultural and economic respects should increase the likelihood of walls being built. A cursory survey provides evidence of this (the EU can be seen as the prototype), but a more precise analysis shows that geopolitical and historical factors must also be considered. Ultimately, the hypothesis of homophily mainly applies to a cluster of (wealthy) Western democracies, which – like a club – maintain low-threshold borders between themselves and instead unite in closing their outer borders. In regions with poorer, mainly undemocratic states, the openness decreases. At the same time, it becomes apparent that autocratically ruled countries often reinforce their borders, as part of strategies of self-assertion relying on the police and the military. There is no satisfactory answer to the question of cultural and religious differences: sometimes they are important, sometimes they are not. On the one hand, it is possible to observe border intensification at the edges of cultural areas; on the other, this pattern should not be overstated, since it is too often interrupted or contradicted. Most new walls, for example, do not separate a Christian 'cultural area' from a Muslim one, but have been built between countries with predominantly Muslim populations.[18]

The hypothesis of homophily is a much better fit for the question of socioeconomic inequality: walled borders are often 'borders of prosperity'.[19] In many cases, then, the reasons for building up borders have more to do with political economy than security policy. Walled borders often appear where there are wealth disparities; they become 'lines of discontinuity',[20] stabilizing economic disparities between neighbouring areas.

Wherever great wealth disparities exist, we see a rise in – to use an economic term – negative externalities, such as unwanted migration movements and human trafficking. The richer countries then build fortified borders to defend themselves against these phenomena. From a statistical point of view, wealth disparities are the most convincing explanatory factor for the existence of walled borders.[21] The more unequal the neighbouring nation-states, the more likely it is that the wealthier side will see itself as negatively affected by border crossings and will try to protect its own territory from them.

The new border management strategy of wall-building can – at the very least – be understood as a direct reaction to the globalization-induced increase in the circulation of people and goods across borders; as I see it, the two elements actually belong together.[22] Walls and globalization appear to go hand in hand, a surprising misalliance at first glance but less puzzling on closer inspection. Contrary to what has frequently been suggested, the intensified circulation of goods and persons does not lead to a straightforward opening of the border, but simultaneously causes selective border closure. Ulrich Beck has argued convincingly that the question of inequality is debordered under conditions of globalization, and no longer stops at the 'national garden fence'.[23] This gives rise to new strategies of inequality management. Walls then become what might be termed the collateral structures of the globalization of opening, serving to stabilize and reproduce thresholds of inequality.

And yet walls of inequality cannot be explained solely by the relationship between two neighbouring countries; they may also relate to other, more distant regions and events that trigger mobility. If globalization means that different and distant places become interconnected and react to one another, then the new walls are definitely part of it. In this context we speak of the polycontexturality[24] of borders – admittedly a rather awkward term from the language of sociology. Thus the Hungarian border fence ostensibly follows a traditional logic of separation with regard to Serbia's territory, but on closer observation it proves to be part of developments in EU border and migration management, without which it would not have been built. It is in part a reaction to the humanitarian crisis in Syria, the highly problematic Dublin agreement, and the precarious political relationship between the EU and Turkey.[25] For refugees on the Balkan route, the border fence between Serbia and Hungary is just one of the many obstacles on the way to a destination country. It is a border that is embedded in a supraregional, if not global, constellation: part of a whole cascade of borders. Despite rigid control and the use of the military to enforce security, however, this border has remained permeable for citizens of neighbouring Serbia.[26]

Walls can be understood as a kind of 'authoritative display of control at the border',[27] that is, as a manifestation of state authority, which is concentrated at the border because it is particularly visible there. Concrete walls, watchtowers, chain-link fences and barriers lend a physical-material reality to the state's aspirations to control and power. At the same time, their architectural design speaks the language of defence, which still focuses on territory and the enclosure of spaces.[28] In concrete terms, this is about marking and defending territorial sovereignty over the exclusion of migrants, and about the enforcement of geopolitical interests and national security needs, extending to the political functions of 'othering' and symbolic demarcation.

Research on the build-up of walls and border barriers has repeatedly stressed that these structures generate a specific symbolic order: 'in front of the wall' versus 'behind the wall'. The wall has a performativity that goes beyond its mere sorting function.[29] Walls obstruct people's view and allow the collective psyche to feel simultaneously cut off and protected. Divisions of space by means of walls give permanent form to the territorial segregation of the 'others': everything behind the wall can categorically be classified as foreign and threatening. Former US President Donald Trump used these motifs again and again, in an unsubtle and deliberately malicious manner, denouncing Mexicans as drug dealers, criminals and rapists to justify his wall-building project. Threat, foreignness, inferiority and non-belonging are the associative contexts of walled borders. Walls lend material form to the need for protection and security, but also to racist and nativist attitudes.

Traditional fortifications such as forts often functioned as outposts in an environment perceived as hostile: outside the enclosure lay the 'uncivilized wilderness' or the enemy. A similar dichotomous order can also be created by walls: the zone of security and belonging sets itself apart from an environment marked as different and therefore threatening, thus imputing otherness to what is found behind the border. The construction of border fences and border walls marks a difference – not just objectively, but also in cognitive perceptions and notions of order. Here the militarization of the border can contribute to a situation where 'others' are perceived less and less as human beings, and more and more as potential threats.

Politically, walls often function as a strategically deployed antidote to a discursively produced danger. There is no better illustration for this than the visits by Donald Trump to trade fairs where large construction companies vied for lucrative contracts to build a ten- to thirty-metre-high wall along the US-Mexican border. Being enclosed generates feelings of security (but also, paradoxically, the opposite: an atmosphere of danger), regardless of whether it can really reduce the risks of terrorist attacks and 'uncontrolled immigration'. At the same time, treating the border wall as a crucial, existential issue paves the way for a kind of politicization, based on the distinction between 'us' and 'the others', which is used by certain political forces to mobilize their own supporters. The wall allows distinctions to be made between friend and foe, and not just externally, but also internally: now opponents of the wall or those sceptical towards it can also be presented as potential threats to the nation. The situation in Hungary has been similar since Viktor Orbán pushed through the construction of a 'southern border fence' on the border with Serbia. This border is a core component of his political ambitions, which go hand in hand with the dismantling of democratic achievements and a narrowing of Hungary's political culture. Like Trump, Orbán has used the issue of migration to build up a sense of threat, and has presented himself as a saviour, rescuing the nation from the 'invasion' of refugees and/or migrants. It speaks volumes that the billboards near the border urging refugees to return to their home countries were written in Hungarian, not in Arabic, Kurdish or Dari. Clearly their main target audience is Orbán's voters.

Wendy Brown has described the political symbolism invested in walls as 'theatre', used by the state to conceal its actual loss of control, and to disguise the fact that the sovereignty of modern statehood has long since been destabilized by processes of globalization and debordering.[30] She argues that the new border walls and fences do not reflect the state's omnipotence and unwavering strength; instead, they are structures of weakness, signs of the erosion of state sovereignty. It is true that the height and solidity of a wall should not be taken as evidence of the extent of state sovereignty. However, the hypothesis that border walls are purely symbolic in nature and therefore basically ineffectual is far too simplistic. Wherever we look, the world's walls are powerful instruments of territorial separation, and of the filtering and sorting of mobility.

Fortified borders can have a substantial filtering and blocking effect on those who are 'unwelcome', leading to the development of camps at many of these borders (as well as elsewhere). These camps themselves have infrastructure typical of borders – for example perimeter fences. They do not always spring up outside the border, but sometimes form indentations into the territory on the other side, where they are subject to special legal conditions. In these places, people gather or are brought together (this includes forms of deportation and forced movement), and are then 'immobilized' indefinitely. They live in precarious circumstances, with an unclear legal status, unequal treatment by the police and the administration, and subhuman social and hygienic conditions.[31] Often these sites arise from bottlenecks, blockages or refusals of entry, situations in which people are not permitted to cross the border, but are, for various reasons, not able to return. It is estimated that there are more than 10 million people worldwide living in refugee camps and informal settlements because of displacement, expulsion and migration: Burmese refugees in Thailand and Bangladesh, people from Venezuela in Colombia, Syrians in Turkey, Somalis in Kenya, Africans in Ceuta. The political and humanitarian disaster of the Moria refugee camp on the Greek island of Lesbos has forced the European public to stop looking the other way, and to see what has become the reality of life for many people on the fringes of the EU: a desperate and exhausting struggle to arrive and to survive, an indefinite wait in limbo.

Many of these camps have arisen in direct response to spatial and physical barriers which stop people from moving on. They are the shunting stations of world politics. If there an increase in migration and a simultaneous increase in border fortification, then bottlenecks and stoppages – the situations in which camps are formed – will become more likely. One such encampment is the 'Calais Jungle', a city of tents on a former landfill site, where several thousand people gathered in 2015 and the following years before attempting to reach Britain. The inhabitants resisted the efforts of the French authorities to clear the camp, and used this as a basis to build networks and act collectively. This was about defending the status quo, in the hope of eventually progressing further. Other transit camps on the so-called Balkan route, for example at the Serbian-Hungarian border or the Turkish-Greek border, show similar characteristics.

Often, however, these separate spaces are the product of political strategy: politicians hope to be able to concentrate the 'problem' of 'placeless people' locally and make it administratively manageable. The authorities are even able to transform 'wild' or 'spontaneous' camps into a form of confinement, including specific 'emergency architecture'. This results in 'total institutions', in some cases secured by the police, which contain and assimilate the people they house. For the Italian philosopher Giorgio Agamben, camps are laboratories of total power, and emblematic manifestations of 'bare life' (*la vita nuda*), because they enforce subordination, restrict the individual's freedom of action and movement, and suspend the possibility of political participation.[32] People are at the mercy of these camp conditions; leaving the camp entails considerable personal risks. It is not by chance that some camps are governed by special legal provisions, which separate them from the territories where they are located. From the perspective of the border, they can be viewed as internal exclusions – as islands of restricted rights. This is particularly obvious when, for example, access to asylum is restricted or inhabitants are not permitted to leave the camp.

Both individually and institutionally, camps close to borders are associated with a promise of temporariness: individually because many inmates hope that the camp will only be a transit point on their journey; institutionally because the structure and the concept of the camp suggest that it will eventually be dismantled.[33] Often both these expectations are in vain: we know many examples of camps that have been transformed into settlements or residential areas, with schools, shops and regular postal addresses, as though the state of emergency had been made permanent. The transition from an interim solution to a permanent state is obviously fluid, but becomes apparent from certain indicators such as the construction of perimeter fences, the codification of rules for entering and leaving, modes of registration, the presence of administrations and organs of control, and the long-term deployment of aid agencies. Life in the camp is thus organized and formalized in the medium and long term, and, in a sense, assumes the character of a regime. In parallel to these technologies of power imposed from the outside, and aimed at regulation, administration and provisioning, diverse forms of self-organization also emerge, including both mutual assistance and the development of hierarchies and social control. In the camps, repressive and controlling elements are linked very closely and in a very specific way with the politics of provisioning – often they become impossible to separate.

Today such camps are – even if it sounds cynical – a self-evident component of closed border regimes. Their political creation and their administration are state strategies to cope with and manage irregular migration. It becomes clear here that refusing people entry at a border leads to new enclosures and special zones. For those who are accommodated in these camps, the spatial concentration and separation makes it plain that they are meant to be prevented from participating in the 'normal' social life taking place outside the camp's gates or fences. As a bottleneck zone at a closed border, the camp becomes a container for those who have no secure residence permit in a particular territory. Or if it springs up behind the border, it becomes an enclave within a territory, an enclosed and fenced special zone, reflecting the functions of the border inside the country and restricting people's movements.

5

Filtering Borders: Granting Unequal Opportunities for Mobility

Sometimes borders that seemed to be open just a moment ago can suddenly close again. British citizen Richie Trezise had accepted a job in Auckland, New Zealand, but in autumn 2007 the authorities there refused entry to him and his wife Rowan. The reason was that the couple had been weighed and found to be too heavy. The girth and body mass index of the would-be immigrants were above the upper limits for new arrivals, and it was feared that the two heavyweights would prove too costly for the health system. The couple subsequently joined a weight loss programme and managed to squeeze through the half-open door to happiness. Dutch citizen Hans Paul Verhoef was even more unfortunate when he landed at an airport in Minnesota in 1989: the well-known AIDS activist was arrested and detained for five days after US border guards found the drug AZT in his luggage. At the time people who were HIV positive were considered to be an 'exceptional risk'.[1]

Were these isolated cases of health-based classification and sorting? Certainly not! People applying for a visa to Pakistan are asked for their blood group; Japanese consulates enquire about applicants' history of drug use; many countries demand proof of vaccination or an HIV test before granting visas. Despite a UN agreement to abolish restrictions on travel for those testing positive for HIV, there are still forty-eight countries worldwide that impose such limitations.[2] And finally, the Covid crisis has been the ultimate in global health-related border closures, putting the question of health status, vaccination certificates and tests at the border onto the political agenda. In spring 2020, no fewer than 186 countries introduced restrictive measures at their borders to contain the pandemic and prevent the entry of those infected with the virus.[3]

During the Covid crisis, questions of health and borders came to be connected as never before. At first, the idea of linking people's freedom of movement with their health and immunity status was laughed off as absurd, but within just a few months this became worldwide political practice. Cold symptoms, a cough and a raised temperature were taken as indications of a possible infection, potentially leading to refusal of entry at the border or the imposition of a quarantine. Many countries introduced travel bans for people from countries with high infection rates.

The connection between chains of infection and borders seems obvious, even if the World Health Organization (WHO) itself was cautious about recommending border closures in the early stages of Covid-19. A frequently cited study in the scholarly journal *Nature* in 2006, on the connection between the spread of influenza and border closures, calculated that border restrictions, even if they managed to reduced travel by over 90 per cent, would at best succeed in delaying the spread of the illness by two to three weeks.[4] More recent studies do see border closures and travel restrictions as effective containment measures, if they are introduced early.[5] Nonetheless, not all countries reacted in the same way. The specific measures taken and the extent of border closures were linked with the general border policies of each country: the more elaborate the infrastructure at border crossings, the more robust the border fortifications, and the tighter the control exerted by the border police, the more rigorous were the border closures during the pandemic.[6]

Some people may be surprised to hear that health issues are relevant to borders, but this is by no means a new development. Border protection and health protection are a long-established double act: the quarantining of goods or persons to combat the plague was first heard of in the twelfth century and was generally practised from the seventeenth century onwards. They are also a fixed component of the external relations of states and of international agreements. The mid-nineteenth century, for example, saw the start of a series of international health conferences, the International Sanitary Conferences (regarded as precursors to the modern WHO), aimed at the transnational coordination of quarantine measures. Cholera and yellow fever were spreading across borders, and people arriving in France, Italy or England from 'risk areas' were placed in camps as a precaution. Soon there was an international patchwork of different approaches to infectious diseases. This frequently led to intergovernmental animosities, because the conditions for entry varied substantially from country to country. Many travellers found themselves – after a short trip across the Channel – stuck for over a month on a quarantine ship anchored off the coast of England, as a preventative measure by the port authorities. Supply chains were interrupted, cargoes of food were spoiled, deliveries did not reach their addressees or arrived much too late. Some countries used quarantine measures deliberately to eliminate competition. In the end, international traders pushed for uniform international standards in the interests of commerce.

In those days, travel was by ship or by land. With the rise of passenger air travel, questions of health policy became more acute. In 1934 it still took eight days and more than fifteen stops to fly from Singapore to London by propeller-driven plane, but even these early flights were accompanied by fears about the introduction of insects or pathogens from afar (the 'mobility of disease').[7] The more air travel increased, the more the authorities worried that malaria or yellow fever might spread unnoticed in their own country. Much thought was therefore given to protective measures, such as putting passengers in quarantine, or making them pass through pesticide-impregnated curtains and nets before getting on and off the plane, to stop mosquitoes from joining the flight. The exponential rise in border crossings, the acceleration of travel and the increasing range of mobility are obviously important drivers of the rapid and global spread of infectious diseases. After the first cases have appeared in a particular place, the pathogens often reach the other end of the world at incredible speed on board a Boeing or an Airbus. Today the planet has become a condensed epidemiological space: extremely distant locations can be reached by plane even before the end of the incubation period prior to the onset of the disease.

There has been extensive research and documentation on body-related border policies designed to protect against illness and pathogens. There is a very obvious tendency to associate health risks with the stigma of the foreign: illnesses invade a state's territory and its population from outside, they are 'exotic' dangers. From this perspective, it is logical for states to differentiate between those they identify as the sources of danger, and their own 'safe' and 'healthy' citizens. 'Foreigners' as the actual or presumed bearers of illnesses have often been ostracized, persecuted and excluded. Labelling SARS-CoV-2, or Covid-19, as the 'Chinese virus' is symptomatic of this. Attributing the origin or cause to a distant location (outside one's own national borders) suggests a potential political answer: to avert dangers by closing borders and preventing mobility. It is not by chance that an important term in border studies, the *cordon sanitaire*, comes from the fight against epidemics. Its literal meaning is the creation of an area of isolation, but today it is often used for border regions or for buffer zones between states involved in conflict.

The sovereign nation-state is always, in part, a biopolitical actor. One indicator of this is a development from the late eighteenth century, the institutionalization of public health authorities (in German *Gesundheitspolizei* or 'health police'), with their own personnel and their own statutory duties. In historical population policies, the monitoring of infectious diseases, the control of migration and the idea of a homogeneous (and healthy) nation were always closely intertwined. National public health policy saw it as its duty to protect the health of the nation (*Volksgesundheit*). This has always included border policy instruments such as the notification of diseases or contacts, interviews, medical diagnosis at the border, the ordering of examinations, proof of vaccinations, or cognitive tests.[8] As well as coding people as healthy or unhealthy and assessing medical symptoms, however, the border filter makes use of even more comprehensive risk categories. In the past, people from different origins have also been classified according to whether they were 'clean', 'hygienic' or 'civilized', with the grammar of exclusion focusing on imagined cultural customs and ways of life. It comes as no surprise that racist codes are deeply inscribed in these registers of health-related purity. The connection between the *cordon sanitaire* and racially motivated border policy is a close one.[9]

Even in the age of global movements, the labelling of bodies and persons has been repeatedly reproduced as an integral part of border-related health management in many states.[10] Instead of restricting themselves to the immediate border, states have built up extensive detection and monitoring systems, so as to be able to react promptly to possible risks – either autonomously or in concert with others, within the framework of international and supranational organizations such as the WHO or the European Centre for Disease Prevention and Control (ECDC). The term 'epidemic intelligence' refers collectively to activities concerned with the early detection and evaluation of infectious disease events, using (among other things) virtual and web-based tools and big data mining. Such early warning systems are especially aimed at detecting health risks outside a country's borders, then introducing measures to contain the threat and protect the domestic population.

At first glance, the 'travelling disease' and the containment of health risks appear to address a very specific aspect of border management. On closer inspection, however, the distinction between healthy and unhealthy hints at a general function of borders, which can be expanded to categories such as risky or risk-free, dangerous or harmless, desirable or undesirable. Plainly these are not objective distinctions, but sociopolitical constructs, which are negotiated in various ways, challenged, and constantly reinterpreted. Modern risk policy, as argued by my colleague Andreas Reckwitz,[11] is a policy of negativity, which aims to prevent or at least alleviate conditions regarded as undesirable and problematic. The border, border protection and border control play a special part in risk policy: the exclusivity of the territory means that perceived threats – be it irregular migration, cross-border crime, a virus or terrorism – appear to be spatially separable (and therefore controllable). Risk policy at the border targets anything coming from outside which is identified as a potential risk factor. It comes into play as soon as it is impossible to accurately assess what problems the unimpeded entry of a particular person or group of people might bring. It operates preventatively, by classificatory risk assessment, to foresee and thereby exclude the occurrence of negative effects.

As stated above, the concept of risk can be subject to different political interpretations and instrumentalizations, since it is based on the possible and not the actual occurrence of a negative event. Neither Mr and Mrs Trezise nor the AIDs activist Verhoef were refused entry because of a concrete offence, but because they were classified as a risk. What is seen as a risk can undergo substantial fluctuations, since 'risk realities' are the product of social, political and cultural factors.[12] At the same time, this means that many things can be politicized as risks. Health can be a risk, along with crime, terrorist threats, visa abuse, irregular entry and illegal residence, a lack of health insurance, political activism or financial hardship – basically the list can be extended indefinitely.

According to the Copenhagen School of Security Studies,[13] the concept of risk can be used to rationalize extensive countermeasures, because it always invokes a state of emergency. Policies of border reinforcement rely on the frequent evocation of scenarios of threat, in order to justify and normalize drastic measures.[14] As soon as an event or a group can be understood, framed and rhetorically addressed as a threat, the paradigm of security takes centre stage. The border is the ultimate site of securitization, because this is where risks can be kept 'outside' and excluded. From a security perspective, the dominant rationale is to let in as little as possible and to control as comprehensively as possible. This rationale is only reined in when other considerations intervene, such as the need for economic exchange, civil liberties or tourism. It is diametrically opposed to the imperative of freedom of movement, which calls for a general right to mobility, a right that should only be restricted under certain conditions.

As explained at the outset, the order imposed by the border is always twofold: on the one hand territorial, since it separates spatial compartments from one another and divides the surface area; and, on the other hand, mobility-related, since it selectively permits or prohibits cross-border mobility. Borders as sorting machines serve to differentiate between desirable and undesirable forms of circulation. The territorial order is relatively stable, simply because states and their territories exist and are recognized. The filtering function, however, shows a high degree of historical and comparative variation, so the question of who is allowed to cross the border becomes crucial. Today very few borders worldwide are at the extreme poles of a continuum between complete openness and complete closure. Most borders are like semipermeable membranes: only certain elements (here, categories of persons) can pass through them. This book argues that their filtering function is reinforced in globalization. At first glance they are becoming more open; at second glance more selective; at third glance more rigid – depending on what groups we are talking about. When examining borders and their modes of operation, then, we need to focus on (in the words of sociologist Stephan Lessenich) the 'unequal structures of entitlement within global mobility'.[15]

Because borders are instruments and places of social sorting and risk classification, crossing the border is often fraught with tension for many people. Those wishing to cross are at the mercy of the state's suspicions; they can be X-rayed, searched and questioned, detained or turned back, scanned and frisked. The state's extensive access to the traveller's body means that border controls are always situations of helplessness and powerlessness. The universal logic of the border control is an exchange: the individual grants state authorities extensive rights of intervention and control in exchange for opportunities for entry or mobility. As stated above, not everyone is affected in the same way and to the same extent: (attributions of) risk play a decisive role, along with origin, skin colour, status and passport.

The act of approaching a checkpoint is strictly formalized, as is the examination and questioning that ensue. Deviations from the prescribed mood of solemnity, such as laughing, singing or making jokes, are forbidden, as they could challenge the state's authority and the personnel mandated to represent it. Anyone who does not conform can be reprimanded and potentially subjected to additional control procedures. Away from the regular queues, further searches and interviews take place in separate rooms. Here the border officials can exercise considerable discretion, since they act preventatively on the basis of a suspicion, rather than reacting to an observed deviation from the rules. The border interview can also be understood as a disciplinary rite of transition or of entry. The interview itself is often superficial and meaningless, but it bears a certain resemblance to confession – Mark Salter speaks of a 'confessional complex' because of the interrogatory situation and the obligation to tell the truth.[16]

Of course, it is not possible to judge the selectivity of the border simply by looking at the control procedures at checkpoints. The displacement of border control – away from the border – ensures that the filter only affects a small proportion of travellers at the checkpoint itself. Only in exceptional cases do people crowd around the entry points to a territory, waiting to be let in – examples are the dramatic scenes at the borders to Colombia and Brazil during the mass exodus from Venezuela in 2019, or the thousands of refugees from Honduras at the beginning of 2021, who were obstructed on their way to the US by Guatemalan security forces using tear gas and truncheons. These are striking images which remain fixed in the collective memory, but they are only the tip of the iceberg. In contrast, the sorting process that takes place before people approach the border is wrapped in a cloak of bureaucracy and therefore less obvious. Selectivity is already at work when people stay at home because they feel they have no hope of ever being able to cross any border, or when they apply for a visa and are turned down.

When it comes to the selectivity function, we must first distinguish between mobility and migration. The former comprises the totality of border crossings, be they tourist journeys, business trips or travel for seasonal employment. The latter is a subset of the former and involves longer-term relocation to another country. Empirically, the question that arises is whether borders have become more open or more closed in this respect over time, and – in terms of their filtering function – for whom. When it comes to migration, the absence of systematic data – on a global scale and covering a substantial period of time – makes it extremely difficult to answer this question. Existing individual findings on migration movements are contradictory and not always conclusive; there is a huge discrepancy between countries, and Western countries are certainly not the most open. Forced migration as a consequence of the Syrian civil war, for example, showed that the willingness to admit refugees does not follow the dividing line between liberal and illiberal states, but runs right through it. Syria's neighbour, Turkey, admitted 3.6 million people; Germany took around 750,000; Poland, which has consistently rejected a European quota system for refugees, only accepted around 500; and Israel categorically refuses to admit Syrian refugees.

As far as labour migration is concerned, there are systematic comparative studies for the OECD world at least. However, indications of a liberalization of migration policy, driven by case law,[17] contrast with hints of a growing restrictiveness due to right-wing populism.[18] Quantitative studies show a relaxation in some areas such as labour migration or family reunification, but greater restrictions to prevent irregular migration.[19] At the same time, there is increasingly unequal treatment of different groups. Conditions of entry for highly qualified migrants have been lowered, while those with low qualifications face higher obstacles.[20]

When it comes to immigration, points systems are becoming more and more popular, at least in the Western world. They are regarded as effective instruments of needs-based management, aimed at harmonizing demand in domestic labour markets with the qualifications and potential of migrants. The evaluation takes into account age (the younger the better), qualifications (the higher the better), work experience (the more the better) and language skills (the more extensive the better). Often assessors also produce a forecast of the candidate's prospects of integration, which essentially means his or her prospects on the labour market. One argument cited to support the use of points systems is the international competition for skilled workers: each country wants to attract and cream off the most able candidates in the hope of strengthening the domestic economy. The risk inherent in this blatant utilitarianism is the possible failure of integration. In many countries – Canada is just one example – applicants create online profiles and are automatically evaluated on the basis of different criteria. If they attain a minimum score, they are transferred to a pool of candidates, ranked by the number of points awarded. In some countries, employers can express specific recruitment interests, which can improve candidates' scores. Since immigration is subject to quotas, only the 'most able' applicants are considered – i.e., those with the highest number of points.

This kind of cherry-picking is not just seen as legitimate, it is frequently held up as a model for other countries. The state's interest in selecting migrants on the basis of its own considerations of utility proves to be in harmony with the right to national self-determination. It also coincides with the idea of the state as a cooperative alliance focused on mutual benefits, which is not only free to decide whether to accept new members, but is entitled to choose those who promise to deliver the greatest added value. In the case of seasonal work, these may be groups at the lower end of the social hierarchy. During the Covid crisis, for example, Romanian asparagus pickers and meat workers were – despite border closures – not only exempt from German travel restrictions, but had special direct flights organized for them. An 'airlift for asparagus helpers' brought workers from Cluj in Romania to Frankfurt so as not to jeopardize the harvest.[21] In this case (as in many others), economic considerations trump possible health risks – a clear indication of how mutable and arbitrary risk classifications are, and how differently risks and benefits can be weighed against one another.

The risk imperative is even more influential in the case of short-term mobility. To understand this, we must first take a detour via the role of citizenship, since this is what determines whether travellers are perceived as low risk and trustworthy or not. Citizenship not only signals belonging and secures access to a number of rights; a passport also indicates one's place in a global hierarchy of mobility. For most people, the 'birthright lottery'[22] determines what living conditions they will experience and what opportunities they will have in life. Usually, citizenship is not an 'elective attachment', or an optional affiliation that can be chosen according to individual preferences. It is something given to us at birth, to which – in the vast majority of cases – we remain inextricably connected (investor Warren Buffett once spoke of a 'sperm lottery'). Since children cannot choose their parents, we tend to see this attachment to our citizenship as natural, as a principle of descent determined by fate. Since membership of a state is handed down via one's parents or place of birth, children in wealthier countries are advantaged by birth, while those born in poorer countries have – from the outset – much less chance of a life of prosperity and safety. The institution of citizenship embodies legally codified forms of inclusion and exclusion with a high social impact.[23] Within the horizon of the world society, it is citizenship that determines people's living conditions, not individual achievement, as claimed by the paradigm of meritocracy. Regardless of talents and individual achievements, it makes a massive difference whether one is born in the Congo or in Luxembourg, in Afghanistan or in Sweden.

To assess how much this hereditary effect of citizenship affects people's economic conditions, the economist Branko Milanović, in his analyses of global income inequality, has distinguished between a 'location component' and a 'class component'.[24] What interests him is what proportion of global inequality can be attributed to the country one lives in, and what proportion is due to income differences within countries. In other words, is citizenship or class affiliation more important for the enjoyment of (or exclusion from) economic privileges? His calculations show that the wealth gap between countries hardly made any difference 200 years ago. Back then, only 20 per cent of global inequality could be explained by the 'location component' – i.e., country of birth was less important than class. After that, the picture was gradually reversed, and, in the middle of the last century, the 'location bonus' accounted for 80 per cent of global income inequality, while 'class' – the extent of inequality between people born in the same country – explained only 20 per cent. With the rise of

China and India, this correlation has weakened, but even now the global distribution of inequality resembles a feudal society rather than a class society, still less a meritocracy.

Here it should be noted that the principle of location is a core element of the principle of citizenship: in each case citizenship relates to a country, a territory, a nation-state framework. For most people, country of birth and citizenship are identical. A direct or indirect reference to territory is present in both the principle of descent (*ius sanguinis*) and the principle of birthplace (*ius soli*), as well as in the acquisition of a (new) citizenship. All citizens have the right to reside in their 'own' country, and to return there as often as they want. Changing citizenship, on the other hand, is a long and difficult process, often requiring a considerable period of residence in the relevant country. Most countries create substantial obstacles to restrict access to citizenship, or select only those likely to make an economic contribution. Over time there has been a discernible paradigm shift in citizenship policies. The notion that granting citizenship is a form of support that facilitates successful integration has been super-seded by the opposite idea: that it is the culmination of a successful effort at integration – 'earned citizenship', so to speak.[25] The requirements for naturalization – tests of knowledge and language proficiency, economic status, assimilation or cultural fit – thus become indicators of successful integration, for which citizenship is the promised prize.[26]

The sale of 'golden passports' offers wealthy individuals a much less arduous path to a new citizenship. 'Citizenship by investment' programmes[27] are not only to be found in the world's tax havens, but also closer to home: countries such as Cyprus, Portugal and Austria roll out the red carpet for the rich – known in bankers' jargon as 'high-net-worth individuals' – and their families. Passports from EU member states are in particularly high demand, since they confer all the rights of EU citizenship: the right to reside and settle anywhere in the EU, to start up businesses, open bank accounts and enjoy visa-free travel. For those who do not wish to become citizens, similar advantages can be acquired with a long-term residence permit. No fewer than thirteen EU countries offer residence permits for the wealthy.[28] Most beneficiaries of golden passports or residence permits come from Russia, China, Cambodia, Iran, Malaysia or Kenya. The oligarch Roman Abramovich took, in addition to his Russian one, Israeli citizenship in 2018, and became a Portuguese – and thereby EU – citizen in 2021. Peter Thiel, Silicon Valley guru and founder of PayPal, received New Zealand citizenship after just a few short visits. He was welcomed as an ultra-rich individual, and welcomed even more warmly when he donated to an earthquake appeal and purchased luxury properties – even though he had no intention of either living in the country permanently or moving his businesses there. Citizenship, once a stable form of affiliation with substantial cultural and social prerequisites, has become a 'marketable asset' with a price tag (the usual sums range from US$100,000 to US$5 million).[29] Cyprus, a country with a gross domestic product (GDP) of just over 20 billion euros per year, has made more than 6 billion euros with these transactions since 2013.[30] It is estimated that a third of the world's wealthy individuals have a second passport, or dual citizenship,[31] because of the locational benefits this confers.

These benefits can be diverse. At a time when goods and capital move freely around the globe, 'flexible citizenships'[32] are used by investors, wealthy individuals and members of elites to secure greater freedom to choose the locations and affiliations that will suit their investments and lifestyles. The choice of citizenship is influenced by factors such as legal security, tax benefits, physical security, healthcare, climate, a pleasant environment for the family, and educational opportunities, but a particularly significant factor is the associated mobility privileges. The passport a person holds opens doors to other countries, allows participation in a global society, and is the most important filtering criterion for permitting cross-border mobility. The power of passports is unequally distributed across the globe: different citizenships can have very different door-opening, or rather border-opening, effects. Some passports allow the holder to cross borders more or less without hindrance, as a welcome visitor with mobility privileges. Other passports have a stigmatizing effect, making travel difficult and excluding their holders from mobility rights, regardless of their individual qualities. The bearers of certain passports are marked out as objects of suspicion and control, right at the bottom of the global hierarchy of unequally distributed mobility rights. A passport or citizenship can be understood in a Bourdieusian sense as a kind of 'capital', that is, a resource that can be strategically deployed to pursue individual goals and to consolidate and improve one's own status. It broadens or restricts opportunities for positioning and movement in a transnational or global social space.[33] Thus citizenship can either chain people to a place or release them from it.

Henley & Partners, a 'global citizenship and residence advisory firm' working for high-net-worth individuals, advertises its services with the advantages of visa-free travel that come with particular passports. The firm has even created its own 'Visa Restriction Index', allowing well-heeled clients to assess the mobility value of a passport before purchasing. The company's website states:

A person of talent and means need not limit his or her life and business to only one country. Making an active

decision with regard to your residence and citizenship
gives you more personal freedom, privacy and security.
... In today's globalized world, visa restrictions play
an important role in controlling the movement of
foreign nationals across borders. Almost all countries
now require visas from certain non-nationals who
wish to enter their territory. Visa requirements are also
an expression of the relationships between individual
nations, and generally reflect the relations and status
of a country within the international community of
nations.[34]

So golden passports can essentially be understood as
a form of commercialization of rights to mobility
and freedom of movement. These prospects are
enticing, especially for businesspeople and entrepre-
neurs from countries whose citizens have difficulties in
obtaining a visa. Purchasing an appropriate citizenship
elevates them into members of a globally mobile elite.
Postcolonial scholars and others have pointed out that
many of the only partially independent territories in the
Caribbean have chosen not to fully separate from the
former colonial powers so as not to lose their 'passport
benefits'.[35] French or Dutch citizenship gives privileged
access to visa-free travel, an advantage that people are
reluctant to surrender. Furthermore, some Caribbean
countries are extremely active vendors on the golden
passport market.

Visa requirements are the main instrument used to
regulate, limit and control cross-border mobility; visa
waivers, on the other hand, facilitate this mobility.
After the Second World War, would-be travellers,
or at least those wanting to enter countries in the
Global North, usually had to apply for a visa in the
consulate or embassy prior to travel. As long as traveller
numbers remained low, the administrative burden was
manageable, but this burden increased hugely with
the dramatic rise in travel activities. A universal visa

requirement is an impediment to border crossings, and this has been shown to have negative effects on trade relations, investment activities and tourism.[36] It is estimated that the existence of a visa requirement reduces the number of journeys to a particular destination country by around 70 per cent.[37] It is in the interest of states to promote exchange and allow uncomplicated business and visitor trips; checking individual cases is both contrary to these interests and administratively challenging.

Seen in this light, a universal visa requirement is not compatible with globalization. In contrast, visa waivers are based on generalized trust towards the country of origin or the 'passport country'. The abolition of visa requirements in many countries was an essential prerequisite for the massive increase in cross-border human mobility that has taken place. By waiving visa requirements for the bearers of certain passports, states can concentrate their resources on controlling the 'remainder'. Some European states introduced the first visa waivers as early as the 1950s, but it was mainly in the 1970s and 1980s that this instrument was systematically expanded. The US was a latecomer, and did not begin to establish its first visa waiver programmes until the late 1980s. The average number of visa waivers per country rose by almost a third from the late 1960s to 2010, suggesting that countries were opening up to travellers.[38] In 1980, taking into account all destination countries, three-quarters of the world's population were still reliant on traditional pre-arrival visas, which had to be applied for prior to travel at the consulate or embassy (in contrast, a visa on arrival is often no more than an entry stamp or a prior registration). In 2018, only just over half the world's population needed this type of visa.[39] This is a process of opening and travel facilitation that must give every globalization theorist cause for jubilation.

A convincing measure of the 'strength' of a passport is the number of countries its holders can travel to without a visa. Our own research on the 'global mobility divide'[40] enabled us to show how extremely unequally visa waivers are distributed – and that the global divide has widened over the decades. When it comes to visas, there is not only a global hierarchy of mobility rights, but an unmistakable two-class society: those who enjoy the privilege of mobility and those who are excluded from it. From the end of the 1960s to 2010, we do find, as mentioned above, a general, global expansion of visa waivers (and therefore an increase in travel opportunities), but not all states (and citizens) have been able to benefit from this to the same extent. In fact, travel has actually become more difficult for the inhabitants of many countries (Figure 3 shows that the field was not so sharply polarized at the end of the 1960s, while the present-day distribution of visa waivers resembles a U-shape, with higher numbers at both poles).

The clear winners of this development, then, are the countries of the Global North, while the citizens of numerous African countries now have less access to visa-free travel than in the late 1960s. Initially, the practice of visa waivers was part of foreign and development policy. It did not become a matter of migration policy until the 1990s, and it was only after the terrorist attacks in the US on 11 September 2001 that it also became, most emphatically, a matter of security policy. In the late 1960s and in the 1970s there was actually a relatively liberal practice of visa waivers, which extended to many African and Asian countries. In 1969, for example, citizens of Tunisia, Pakistan and the Gambia enjoyed visa-free travel to significantly more countries than citizens of Israel, Portugal and Chile. Today the reverse is true. In the past, visa waivers were often announced during state visits; they were a symbolic act with relatively minor consequences, since few people

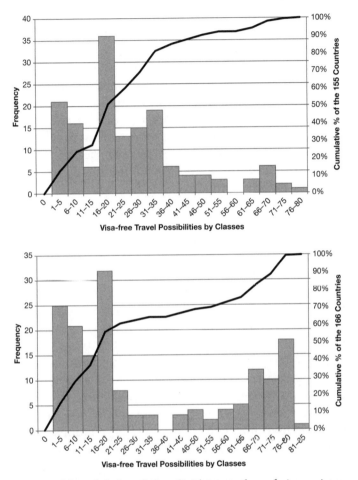

Figure 3: The 'global mobility divide' (number of visa waivers by country, 1969 and 2010)

Notes: Top graph 1969, bottom graph 2010; Visa Network Data; the dataset contains the same 154 countries for both points in time and reflects all visa relations. The graphs show the number of countries (*y* axis) that possess a certain number of visa-free travel opportunities (*x* axis).

Source. Steffen Mau, Fabian Gülzau, Lena Laube and Natascha Zaun, 'The Global Mobility Divide: How Visa Policies Have Evolved over Time', *Journal of Ethnic and Migration Studies*, 41/8 (2015), pp. 1200ff.

travelled. It was only with the rise of tourism and other types of travel – i.e., at the moment when more people began to seize opportunities for mobility – that destination countries became choosier. Overnight, the citizens of many countries found themselves once again having to queue up in front of embassies. In the past twenty to thirty years, the practice of visa waivers in the Global North has become more and more selective.

In our sample of more than 150 countries, the OECD states are currently at the top of the hierarchy when it comes to travel opportunities for their citizens. The front runners are countries such as Denmark, Finland, Germany and Sweden, whose citizens can travel without a visa to more than ninety of the countries in the sample. At the tail end are countries like Afghanistan, Somalia, Cambodia, Ethiopia and Pakistan, whose citizens can only travel to one or two countries without a visa. If we look not at the number of visa-free destinations conferred by each citizenship, but instead consider how open individual countries are to visa-free travel, we see that Western countries are relatively cautious about granting visa waivers, while countries in the regions of East Africa and Southeast Asia are well above the OECD average for visa openness.[41] In the area of visa policies, then, we find thoroughly asymmetrical relationships, in which the Global North has the advantage. The OECD countries – that is, the rich democracies – are able to maximize their own citizens' chances of mobility while remaining relatively closed themselves.[42] The principle of reciprocity, always acknowledged as important in international relations, is partially suspended here, and is only observed between OECD members.

The selective attitude of the 'West' towards the principle of openness is also apparent in its approach to Central and Eastern Europe after the collapse of state socialism. Prior to this collapse, the lack of freedom to travel had been a key motive for political discontentment, and numerous Western states had granted the citizens of the 'Eastern bloc' visa-free travel – though few were able to benefit from this. It was all the more disappointing for Central and Eastern Europeans when, after the fall of the wall and the removal of the barbed-wire fences, the West erected a paper wall of application forms and demands for supporting documentation. Austria, for example, imposed visa requirements on Bulgaria in 1989, and on Poland and other countries in 1990, and required travellers to present an invitation and proof of financial resources before entry. West Berlin was confronted with tens of thousands of people from Poland and other East European countries, and pushed for the abolition of visa waivers in 1990. The experience of East European citizens was similar to that of many people from Africa: once they began to take advantage of visa waivers in large numbers, these became a problem and were suspended. The opening of the East was followed by an at least partial closing of the West, which was only reversed with the prospect of EU membership.

Does the 'power of the passport' mainly depend on a country's economic potency, or are questions of politics also relevant – for example, whether a traveller's country of origin is a democracy or a dictatorship? Empirically it appears that the economy and the political system are both important. Wealthy democracies are right at the top of the global hierarchy of mobility.[43] For countries in the bottom half of the global distribution of inequality, however, it hardly makes any difference whether they take steps towards democracy and grant their own citizens civil liberties.[44] In general, more doors are open to citizens of economically potent countries than to those of economically weak countries, regardless of whether they are democratic.

We can examine this type of selectivity from every possible angle, but the results are always the same, and always striking. If we look at the cost of a visa, for example, we find, yet again, that the Global South is at a huge disadvantage. Would-be travellers from the southern hemisphere must not only apply for visas much more often, they must also pay substantially more.[45] If we compare the average sums required to apply for a visa, it becomes apparent that people from Northern or Western Europe only have to pay a fraction (a quarter to a third) of what the visa costs for travellers from many countries in Asia, North Africa or sub-Saharan Africa. As a rule of thumb, the poorer the country of origin, the more expensive the visa for its citizens. This is a clear indication that the fee is intended to deter people from travelling (along with many other rules that make it difficult to successfully apply for a visa). The picture becomes even more distorted – extremely so – if we compare the costs not in absolute terms but in relation to incomes in the relevant countries. On average, a Western European only has to work for 0.14 days to be able to afford a visa, while a person from sub-Saharan Africa has to work 156 times more, a total of 21.85 days.[46] These apparently insignificant data reveal a pattern that we find again and again: the polarization between mobility privileges for some, and high obstacles to mobility for others.

This pattern also applies to visa approvals: here too, people from the countries at the lower end of the hierarchy of unequal mobility rights trail behind.[47] Their refusal rates are high, despite the fact that it is usually only those who believe they have a chance of a positive outcome who apply in the first place. The obstacles built into the application process are substantial. Applicants are obliged to attend an interview at an embassy or consulate in person; download documents from websites and then upload them again; fill in forms and write notes in English (not in their own national language); provide various documents as evidence of their travel plans; present invitations and sponsorships;

and take out health insurance. All these things are subtle and not-so-subtle obstacles to cross-border mobility. The specific documents that must be submitted at the embassies of the Schengen countries include bank statements, credit card documents, employment certificates, tax self-certifications and salary details, to prove that the applicant has strong professional ties to his or her own country. To prove strong family ties to their country (or 'rootedness'), applicants must present marriage certificates, extracts from the population register showing the persons living in their household, the birth certificates of minor children and evidence of property ownership. Sponsorships and invitations can serve as proof of trustworthiness, greatly improving an applicant's status. The embassy checks the documents and assesses the likelihood that the applicant will return to his or her home country. Unsuccessful applicants for a Schengen visa eventually receive very general and nonspecific explanations for the refusal, such as 'Your intention to leave the territory of the Member States before expiry of the visa could not be verified' (reason for refusal no. 9), or 'The purpose and conditions of the intended stay were not proven' (reason for refusal no. 2)

Such harmless-sounding sentences structure global mobility. They determine access rights, unequal opportunities for freedom of movement, and mobility and immobility. The border as a sorting machine allows and prevents mobility simultaneously – thereby creating global disparities arising from unequal opportunities for mobility. So while some people struggle to even leave their own country, and are repeatedly thwarted in their travel plans, others are born with an entry ticket in their hand. In the opening dialogue to Brecht's *Refugee Conversations*, we find the laconic statement that 'the human being is just the mechanical holder for the passport. ... The passport is the main thing.'[48] The inescapable conclusion is that the world may be virtually borderless, but only for the members of affluent societies. Opportunities for crossing borders have undoubtedly increased, but not everyone has benefited. In fact, it can be observed that – depending on region of origin, status and passport – some people's options for mobility have actually decreased.

The Covid pandemic has not reversed this situation. It may have brought restrictions on mobility to all regions of the world, but it is not an equalizer, levelling out differences. The unequal global distribution of the vaccine is so severe, and the delay in access to vaccines in the Global South so great, that the vaccination privileges of the Global North are likely to consolidate the mobility privileges of its citizens for some time to come. Granting freedom of movement and health certificates to people who have been vaccinated means giving an advantage to those who can afford to minimize or exclude health risks. In this epoch-making crisis, a familiar pattern is repeating itself.

6

Smart Borders: Informational and Biometric Control

In January 2019, at the height of the dispute between the Trump administration and the Democrats over the US budget and the $5.7 billion which the president wanted to spend building a wall between the US and Mexico, the *New York Times* ran the following headline: 'The Real Wall Isn't at the Border. It's everywhere and we're fighting against the wrong one.'[1] The message of the article was that walls had long since lost their function in protecting territories and restricting migration. The role of walls is diminishing, the author argued, because new, often invisible barriers are in operation, and virtual borders are becoming more important. Similar arguments underpinned the Democrats' response when Trump attempted to present them as a danger to national security, uninterested in protecting the US population from an uncontrolled influx of migrants. They described walls as medieval constructions, no longer able to help solve the problems of the twenty-first century. Instead they favoured 'smart borders', held up as an effective means of ensuring security.

'Smart borders' is the umbrella term for the use of new digital technologies to monitor borders and control border traffic. It includes a whole arsenal of different technological possibilities, such as databases, algorithmic risk analyses, biometric identification, automated control, sensor technologies, track and trace procedures, video and audio surveillance, thermal imaging, etc. Smart borders follow the logic of non-physical borders, and rely both on permanent surveillance (events at border crossings or in border zones are made observable at all times, independent of human personnel) and on accurate identification and targeting of individuals (physical features are recorded and related to pools of digital information, which then come into effect during border control). One core aim is to use new technologies and database systems to identify mobile individuals as efficiently as possible, carry out security checks, and filter them.[2] Not surprisingly, digitization has given rise to technological optimism about the complete reorganization of operative border surveillance and control. In recent years, many countries have invested large sums in technological border reinforcement, as a way of meeting the all-important post-9/11 security imperative without missing out on their share of the globalization dividend.[3] The promise held out by smart borders is that opening and closure can be seamlessly combined, and need not come into conflict, since precise distinctions can be made between desirable and undesirable circulation. Smart borders supposedly make it possible to gain security without sacrificing openness.

The technological surveillance of border areas involves developments such as the use of drones, radar installations, cameras on mobile platforms, acoustic sensors and thermal imaging systems, all of which can register suspicious movements at or near the border and trigger an alarm. In 2019, for example, the European border protection agency Frontex launched an experimental airship, equipped with thermal imaging cameras and other technological devices, to monitor the maritime area between the Greek island of Samos and the Turkish mainland. Built by Zeppelin, a company based on the shores of Lake Constance, the airship provided real-time data to the Greek coastguard to help manage the deployment of their vessels. But this is not just about video surveillance of border strips, which has been standard procedure for many decades. It is also about combining visual recording with artificial intelligence, enabling computers to completely take over the work of humans in future. There would then be no need for a human observer in a control tower to register a border violation: artificial intelligence can detect conspicuous movements in the border area, distinguish between humans and animals, recognize weather conditions and automatically trigger an alarm if anything suspicious is found in the data structures.

In principle, these technical systems can operate as functional equivalents of traditional barrier borders, and even replace them, but in practice they have so far mainly served as extensions of these traditional borders. At present, the systematic conversion of physical border structures to technology-based border architectures is still limited to isolated cases or individual sections of border; worldwide, there are a dozen pilot projects at different stages of development. In general, technological components are added to existing border infrastructures, but in other cases the use of technology allows surveillance of border areas that were previously inaccessible or could only be secured at great trouble and expense, such as sparsely populated mountain regions or deserts. It is at least conceivable that the combination of visual, sensor-based, infrared and acoustic border surveillance could replace the border as a physical construction in certain areas. Over the next few years, these technologies will become simpler and less costly, enabling states to introduce virtual surveillance of the border area around the entire perimeter of their territory. This would be a technological *cordon sanitaire*, a border strip of digital surveillance, allowing panoptic observation of all movements in the area near the border and algorithmic analysis of the image and motion data. This will make it possible to actually extend the state's control to all border areas, as envisaged in the image of the sovereign territorial state, but in such a way that the situation on the ground seems largely unchanged at first glance. Thus, the border itself becomes invisible, while the people in the border area are made visible by the technology. These 'smartified' borders therefore create asymmetrical relations of transparency, in stark contrast to the fortified borders which use their visibility as a means of intimidation.

The act of crossing borders can also be organized differently with smart technologies.[4] This is particularly apparent at international airports. Individual steps in the checking process have been delegated to machines, identification procedures are now carried out digitally, and biometric recognition processes such as iris scanning and electronic fingerprinting are now standard at many border crossings. The use of smart border solutions at airports not only substantially increases the depth of control; its other new and noteworthy feature is that it allows the filtering function of the border to be calibrated to much higher numbers of passengers. Mass tourism, commuter flights and business trips constitute huge challenges for border control, and the largest airports in the world have to process more than 100 million passengers per year (or had to, before the outbreak of the Covid pandemic). Manual control and intensive individual checks – interviews, manual searches, etc. – are time-consuming. Smart borders promise not only better, but faster checking processes, as they can differentiate very efficiently and largely automatically between desirable and undesirable, or between low-risk and high-risk mobility. Thus the smart border project is always partly about channelling 'good travellers' across the border fluidly and comfortably, ensuring that they scarcely notice the checking process and are not disturbed or deterred in their movement. It is no coincidence that airports display an intimate symbiosis between control and consumption. In the same spirit, a 'Chinese Friendly Airport' initiative was recently launched at Istanbul airport, with special check-in islands, Chinese goods available for purchase, digital welcome activities and full integration of Chinese apps (Weibo and WeChat), all designed to make Chinese travellers feel at home.[5]

New technologies of risk classification make it possible to undertake the desired risk differentiations with ever-increasing speed and precision, so there is no longer an inevitable clash between the security imperative and the need for fast passenger processing. Like the check-in procedure, which is now generally carried out by the passengers themselves, often digitally, border control is becoming a human–machine interaction taking place largely without personnel (except in a supervisory role). This is known as automated border control (ABC). In many European airports, incoming passengers divide into two groups: those who show their passport to a border official in conventional fashion (except for journeys within the Schengen area), and those EU citizens who enter the country with a machine-readable e-passport. In the latter case, the travellers walk up to an electronic gate, where they place their travel document on a scanner, which reads the personal data and the biometric passport photo stored on a chip, and compares this data with current wanted lists. At the same time, the traveller has to stand in the right position and look straight into a camera, which uses facial recognition software to verify whether the person at the gate matches the passport photo. The comparison lasts just three seconds, and the whole procedure is estimated to take thirty seconds. This is mainly due to the slowness of the individuals, not the machines. This type of border crossing combines self-checking and external checking:

the passenger acts as an assistant border guard, helping the automated gates with their work.

Some time ago, the EU began to experiment with 'virtual' border posts. In the first attempts in Latvia and Greece, going by the name iBorderCtrl, an avatar takes over the tasks of the border officials. Once the traveller has scanned his or her passport and has been electronically fingerprinted, an animated border guard appears on the screen and asks about the traveller's itinerary, the reason for the journey and the luggage he or she will be taking. At the same time, a camera observes the traveller's microexpressions (thirty-eight in total), in order to assess – like a lie detector – whether he or she is telling the truth. (Even under George W. Bush, the US government was planning a kind of brain scan at the border, to detect 'hostile intentions' among inbound travellers.) This then serves as the basis for an algorithmically generated 'risk score', though the accuracy rate in the detection of 'high-risk individuals' is disputed. The developers envisage a two-phase system. First the traveller uses a smartphone to upload documents, provide biometric information and take part in a virtual interview. If he or she then actually appears at the border, the system refers back to this data, potentially speeding up the whole checking process considerably. People classed as 'safe' can then enter the EU without further ado, while people with a lower security classification are subjected to intensive checking and additional questioning – or are simply refused entry.

More than forty countries now use variants of smart border technologies. The growth curve for automated borders is steep, and an economically potent 'closure industry' has evolved in this area.[6] SITA, one of the leading IT specialists in the field of 'border solutions', now offers a comprehensive identity management service based on facial recognition. In the SITA Smart Path™

system, both the identity document and the passenger's face is scanned in, and this data accompanies the traveller throughout the journey. Passengers are not required to undergo subsequent checks or present their documents again, for example when boarding, since the system passes on the data and the face can be automatically identified at all the checkpoints. This information can even be transmitted to the next border. Biometric recognition thus becomes the ultimate door-opener; the technologized border is constantly detecting, constantly making connections between the body and the databases at new points of contact. Some airports have already conducted pilot projects with this technology, and it is not inconceivable that authorities in many countries could merge data acquired in this way with the immigration control system, to create – warning: advertising language – a 'global passenger data and identity management trust framework'. SITA promises a smooth border crossing process, allowing passengers (those classified as safe and trustworthy) to pass through all checks non-stop. According to the company's self-description, 'empathy with travellers' and traveller satisfaction are its top priority.[7] Naturally, such marketing presentations do not mention those who are excluded from this unimpeded flow of mobility because they have been linked with a negative identity marker. Nor do they mention data quality issues, which are still substantial.

For some time now, experts have been thinking about global, forgery-proof identification systems, which would unify the many national variants and thus further simplify the whole technical process.[8] At present, part of the development is focused on enhancing the biometric and digital elements of passports. At the same time, there are plans to gather and make available more and more personal information, unconnected to passports. EU regulation 2019/1157 stipulates that fingerprints

– previously used to identify suspects and criminals, and later also refugees – will be stored in all new ID cards as standard. (Interestingly, the rationale links this change with the right to freedom of movement and residence in the Charter of Fundamental Rights, arguing that more secure ID cards are required to protect these rights.) The better that biometric systems work, and the more that information is stored in advance, the less need there is for the passport itself at the smart border. If people can be identified and classified biometrically, paper passports become superfluous. Faces serve as passports – and offer the additional advantage that they can be 'read' routinely and unobtrusively, while a passport always has to be requested. Dubai International Airport has already set up 'smart gates' or 'smart tunnels' (marketed as a 'speedy flow solution' or 'seamless journey'),[9] which utilize a combination of facial recognition and iris scanning to allow automated biometric verification, thus minimizing delays for travellers. Here, checking takes place within fifteen seconds, without any human contact, but also without passports, travel documents or bureaucratic boarding procedures.[10] Similar solutions are found at Beijing Capital International Airport (BCIA), the world's second-busiest airport, which also relies on biometric identity and security management. Passengers register in advance with their mobile device, and later use their smartphone for data verification at the checkpoints. The idea is that – for welcome travellers! – a perfect smart border will work like the automatic glass doors of a department store, which open as soon as you approach, then close silently behind you. At the same time, this putative perfect border will go unnoticed by mobile individuals, becoming a contactless 'walkthrough' border.

In the biometric model of control, the body itself is the bearer of information, which is then duplicated in databases. Because it takes unchangeable physical features as its starting point and does not rely solely on the documents carried by travellers, it is much easier to exclude forgery and manipulation. In contrast to traditional (manual) systems for establishing identity, the decision about identity or non-identity is made by automated processes of calculation and pattern recognition, and is therefore not subject to human decision-making on the ground.[11] These systems are connected to more extensive security infrastructures, aimed at fighting crime, terrorism and irregular migration, which analyse biometric data for forensic and preventive purposes. Some researchers have argued that the border itself is a data extraction point, where people repeatedly allow their identifying information to be gathered by the authorities.[12] At each pit stop on the border, new data can be extracted and connections can be made between the person and the databases. For authoritarian regimes in particular, this is a dream come true: where else do citizens of their own country or other countries submit – routinely and without legal restrictions – to fingerprinting and iris scanning, if not at the border? Some regimes go even further: irregular migrants caught in the US are forced to give a DNA sample, which is then stored,[13] and the Canada Border Services Agency compares its information with commercial databases if there are doubts about a person's origins.

The expansive growth and development of biometric databases also increase the potential for automatic searches and comparisons; sometimes there is even talk of 'bio-bordering'.[14] Of central importance here is the linking of data systems and the sharing of information across national borders. The smart border is part of global data flows and exchanges of information, and it transforms the role of the territory itself, because the digital space creates new connections between the national territory and the world. The digital border loses its reference to a specific location. In the EU, the Prüm Convention has vastly increased opportunities for cross-border retrieval of biometric data. Numerous national databases have been linked up, allowing not only searches for fingerprints and DNA as part of individual enquiries, but also, in future, large-scale searches using (for example) still images from surveillance cameras.

Biometric identification of persons is, however, just one element of the 'smartification' of border control. Another is data-based and algorithmic screening and scoring processes, as in the iBorderCtrl pilot project.[15] As mentioned, each time a person crosses a border more data can be extracted, and records can be expanded and combined, potentially leading to a form of 'dataveillance'.[16] In the past, border control was all about verifying the validity of documents and making sure that the person and passport matched up, but today it is more about accessing information stored in databases. It is therefore possible to speak of the 'datafication' of borders, or 'big borders'[17] (by analogy with 'big data'). This is not just a matter of the information that people submit themselves; rather, information from various databases is combined to draw conclusions about a person's trustworthiness. This can be information about previous travel activities, financial status and also personal information retrieved from social media. The definition of uniform data formats and the enforced use of certain technologies for data sharing create extensive opportunities for access, which can be utilized by different states and their agencies. There are efforts, both in the EU and elsewhere, to connect more and more information, and to integrate travel data, personal information and biometric data to create a 'common identity repository'. This data can be used to make statements about every individual. But the algorithmic analysis of patterns and combinations of characteristics can also serve as the basis for risk classifications – though these have shown substantial rates of error so far.

Many of the new systems are interoperable and link not only different databases but also previously separated areas of society. If it is possible to siphon off data covering many different aspects of people's lives, then this information can also be used to regulate mobility. This means that the surplus of control[18] that is always inherent in digitization, simply because we can scarcely participate in social and economic life without leaving a data trail, can also be deployed to allow or restrict mobility. The social credit system in China offers a telling example. The Chinese government has blocked citizens' access to mobility on the basis of scores given for consumption, political behaviour and social media activities, by imposing travel bans on those who have been blacklisted because of low scores. In 2018 alone, this led to nearly 18 million thwarted attempts to purchase airline tickets, and nearly 6 million citizens were unable to buy tickets for fast trains. The reasons for these travel bans include a wide range of 'sins', such as tax debts, the dissemination of undesirable or false information, smoking in trains, or walking the dog without a lead. Another example of the sharing and use of sensitive data in the context of mobility is an agreement between the Chinese internet platform Alipay and the Canadian government, allowing Chinese tourists to submit their Zhima Credit score as proof of solvency when applying for a Canadian visa. With a score of over 750 (scores range from 350 to 950), users can request an automatic report with information on their financial status, which they can then submit to the Canadian embassy. The Zhima Credit score, however, is more than a simple assessment of creditworthiness. It also takes into account consumer behaviour, preferences, willingness to repay, networks and financial transactions in the past, thus going beyond the narrow financial aspect. A high Zhima score suggests that the bearer is a low-risk and therefore welcome individual. Thus information from a completely different context is being used to determine whether a person is allowed to enter another country. At the same time, the private sector is interacting with a government agency, because it is often the powerful IT firms that have the necessary technological competencies, and not the state. Under Trump, the US introduced the legally disputed regulation that applicants for residence visas had to disclose not just personal data but their social media profiles and contacts from the last five years, e.g., on Facebook, Twitter or Instagram. The authorities hoped that this data will enable them to make more accurate risk assessments. And in Russia there have been reports of plans to make labour migrants install an app that would contain not only the usual personal information, but also their biometric data, state of health and police record. This would allow the state to monitor 'foreigners' and expel them if necessary.[19]

Technology is making it possible to log more and more traces of our lives digitally; this then paves the way for diagnostic risk classification tools targeting the individual. The data shadow hanging over us, which describes and tracks our social, political and economic lives, can easily be used to make algorithmic predictions of behaviour. The aim here is to detect and mark out potentially 'suspect populations' (those with a risk prognosis), in order to restrict their opportunities for movement. The combination of biometrics and algorithmic classification gives rise to a special 'biopower',[20] focused on coding people as 'risks'. In 'predictive analytics', which are now applied in many areas, large quantities of data are analysed in order to predict future events, such as whether someone might become a visa overstayer or not. Here it is not crucial to uncover an incident from the past or to ascertain concrete facts; instead, processes based on probability forecasts lead to risk classifications. The combination of unfavourable 'critical' characteristics or the extrapolation of 'digital scars' can trigger suspicion. When behaviours, preferences and social networks can be analysed on the basis of human interactions with networked digital devices, this creates 'data selves'[21] – i.e., digital reflections of individuals. Naturally, these are also of interest to the authorities controlling the borders. Data mining and algorithmic processes can now calculate much more accurately the construct that these authorities are concerned with: the trustworthy border-crosser. A border built with stones and barbed wire, or with paper and documents, could be replaced by a border drawn with data and algorithms – a classificatory border. If biometric identification is added to the mix, the physical body with its biometric information is combined with the data body.[22]

Voluntary donations of data, such as those incentivized in the 'trusted traveller' programmes established by some countries, are another entry point for the increasingly extensive informational control that can accompany opportunities for mobility. Such programmes invite travellers to register in advance and 'voluntarily' share their own data. In return, if they are assessed as low risk, they benefit from faster processing at the border: data in exchange for mobility. The US firm Clear,[23] which specializes in identity verification, has turned this into a business model, and now works in more than sixty airports in the US. Five million subscribers already pay US$170 per annum to pass security checks faster by disclosing personal data in advance. At the airports they go through special gates that establish their identity with iris or fingerprint scans. Clear is currently expanding its business model far beyond identification, adding personalized data from all areas of life to customer profiles. The idea is to form an even more comprehensive picture of a person's trustworthiness, which can then also secure advantages elsewhere.

While control was previously concentrated mainly on the border of entry, we now observe that controls on mobility can move away from there and become independent of location. Detection of location and time spent there, mobility data, GPS tracking, interaction data and proximity tracing: all these can be made available and analysed. The result is that, depending on the legal structures in which one is operating, control no longer has to be limited to particular places of verification or identification. Security agencies can exert control regardless of whether someone is passing through a checkpoint or not – for example when facial recognition is used for authentication. In this scenario, the control previously located at the border would be diffused into the territory. The surveillance of public spaces and control by border police would no longer be fundamentally distinguishable in terms of the tools they deploy and their objectives of risk prevention: in each case the aim would be to assess and evaluate risks, detect anomalies,[24] and carry out interventions in line with security policy. Identification, surveillance, classification and behaviour prediction would then be general technologies of control both at and beyond the border, but would not be clearly visible for those affected by them.

The example of the 'pandemic border', already cited above, showed us that health risks can become a distinguishing criterion at the border. This is another area where development is being accelerated by smartification, since opportunities for access to health information are expanding. During the Covid-19 pandemic, for example, China very quickly linked internal mobility to a QR code app used at crossing points and entry gates. Those who follow the rules and are considered harmless (healthwise) get a green signal, those with a yellow code are required to go into quarantine, while a red signal indicates that they are infected or come from a high-risk area. They are then (for example) denied access to public transport.

China is a pioneer in this respect, but it is not unique. Many states, tech companies, airlines and travel operators are working frantically to develop programmes that will give digital access to travellers' health and vaccination information.[25] The International Air Transportation Association (IATA) is working on an IATA Travel Pass, a digital platform for passengers. This will not only give access to travel information, but will allow travellers to upload and share their test results and vaccination certificates.[26] Travel apps could bring together passport and health data, and could then be used not just for the border crossing or check-in, but also for contact tracing and quarantine monitoring. Another reason why digital travel documents with biometric identification are seen as advantageous is that they allow contactless control. Since there is no longer any need for a direct exchange of documents, the risks of contagion are minimized. The question this raises, of course, is whether this opens the door to discrimination based on health status – or whether distinguishing between different groups is actually a step forward, since people who are immune or vaccinated should no longer be refused any rights of mobility or other fundamental rights if they have been proven to pose little or no health risk to others.

After the dramatic collapse of the airport business during the height of the Covid-19 pandemic, the above-mentioned US company specializing in identification technology, Clear, shifted its focus to recording health data in its applications. The latest development is an app-based 'health pass', which records whether the holder has Covid symptoms, has tested positive, or is immune or vaccinated. Ultimately, this means that people can use their smartphones, combined with identity verification, to gain entry anywhere. Here, Clear is extending its reach far beyond airport security, aiming to develop a general check-in technology for sports events, business premises, local transport and access to public buildings or universities. This company, originally founded in the wake of the 9/11 attacks, perceives the Covid crisis as a similar impetus for securitization. Unsurprisingly, the latest 'Freedom on the Net' report found that the pandemic has led to more digital surveillance (sometimes referred to as 'biosurveillance') all over the world, as government agencies – for health protection and quarantine monitoring purposes – are now making use of phone and location data, cameras with facial recognition and temperature scanners in public spaces.[27] This has a particularly severe impact on vulnerable groups such as irregular migrants, who are reduced to their physical and health-related characteristics by this digital intervention.[28]

Of course, it is easy to take a critical view of this development, as part of an ongoing datafication of health information. On the other hand, there are also good reasons to tap the full potential of digitization to fight the pandemic. It should be pointed out, however, that the development, deployment and dissemination of such monitoring technologies lead to technological lock-in effects and a lowering of sociopolitical inhibitions. We have rapidly grown accustomed to things that would have been unthinkable a few years ago, such as body scanners, iris scanning and fingerprinting at international airports. The SARS epidemic in 2003 had a major influence on the response to Covid-19 in Singapore and Hong Kong, including the use of advanced screening technologies and contact tracing. At Noi Bai International Airport in Hanoi, thermal scanners were introduced soon after the outbreak of Covid-19, checking incoming travellers for symptoms of fever before the gates opened to let them through. Once technologies have been introduced and tested, they create path dependencies and habitualize their use, making a return to the previous state of affairs unlikely. It is therefore quite conceivable that the future response to any severe outbreak of flu or of another infectious and highly communicable disease will involve similar technological solutions. The feeling of threat, the creation of security and the minimization of risks are, in any case, key reasons why many people accept extensive state surveillance measures despite concerns about privacy.[29] So it can be assumed that the interlinking of health information and mobility will very probably be incorporated into the repertoire of government policies. This implies an intensification of the already established biopolitical coding of the border, with the addition of smart tools. The border as a sorting machine would then use health aspects for risk classification as a rule, and not just in exceptional cases. We cannot yet predict to what extent this will actually happen, but we can be certain that borders will continue to become 'smarter'.

7

Macroterritories: Dismantling Internal Borders, Upgrading External Borders

Over history, empires have played a major, arguably dominant role as forms of large-scale organization of political rule.[1] All empires – be it those of Alexander the Great, Rome or Britain, Mongolia under Genghis Khan or Byzantium – opted for territorial expansion as a way to assert themselves and extend their sphere of influence. Political domination was mainly associated with the enlargement of an empire's boundaries. Some of these empires were short-lived, but others endured for long periods of history. In these cases, substantial efforts were required to maintain territorial cohesion. The relationship between the centre and the periphery was often precarious, and the vast extent of the empire made complete control difficult. In the attempt to prevent the secession of individual provinces, the authorities resorted to military occupation, bureaucratization and the development of transport and trade routes. Eventually, all these empires collapsed, usually because of economic exhaustion or misplaced claims to power, but often because of territorial overexpansion, which allowed centrifugal forces to prevail.

Despite this history of fallen empires, there was a theory popular among historians and geographers before the First World War, the *Weltreichslehre*, or theory of world empires, which asserted that the world was gradually being divided into large regional blocs dominated by 'superstates'.[2] According to the theory, the dominance of individual, large, resource-rich and potent states led to the subordination of other states in their geographical proximity and the redrawing of borders. This did not mean full territorial integration of these countries, but a reduction in their sovereignty. At the time, proponents of this theory were thinking of countries such as Russia, the British Empire and the United States of America, which even Max Weber saw as the new Rome. After the Second World War, a bipolar world order emerged, with the Soviet-dominated eastern bloc on one side and the Western world on the other. Here too, there were signs of imperial structures.[3] But in 1989 this world of blocs also came to an end, signalling for many the start of a new era.

One might think that the story of large imperial territories had come to an end with the collapse and disintegration of the Soviet empire. Even in the 1990s, however, there was already talk of new camps – based on cultures, religions and identities – replacing the old political-ideological blocs. It was suggested that dividing lines were emerging at the points of intersection between cultures – for example, Western, Islamic, Chinese Confucian and Latin American. Samuel Huntington's oft-cited theory of the 'clash of civilizations'[4] asserted that the new geography of separation followed cultural and religious patterns, and that politics and economics were now secondary. The implication of this theory for our questions of mobility and border policies would be that these 'cultural borders' and their cartographic representations are leading to the emergence of new areas of internal opening and external closure. We have already seen, however, in Chapter 4 on fortification, that, while the 'wall around the West'[5] certainly does exist, there are also many fortified borders between culturally similar countries – for example, between

Muslim-majority countries, and not, as one might assume, between Muslim and Christian countries.[6] Nor are cultural factors instrumental in the militarization of borders between Russia and several former Soviet republics (which have been sovereign states since the 1990s), or the walls and fences built by South Africa and Botswana to prevent an influx of migrants from their poorer neighbour, Zimbabwe. So even superficial research shows that a world map based on civilizations has only limited relevance for current questions of territorial borders and mobility.

Nonetheless, processes of border formation should not be viewed solely in terms of individual states, since regional contexts can have a substantial influence on the question of borders and mobility. In a pioneering work of comparative regionalism, Emanuel Deutschmann has shown that regional clusters – which are embedded in global processes of debordering, yet have their own momentum – play a significant role in mobility (of migrants, asylum-seekers, students and tourists).[7] If we compare regionalization and globalization as independent processes, in terms of their relevance for the mobility of people, then regionalism is actually the dominant process. In short, regions matter! Even for globalized Europe, most border crossings occur in a regional rather than an interregional context. This observation also applies to other regions of the world. So regional processes of opening and regional areas of circulation have an important function in the structuring of mobility. In some cases – though we should avoid painting too rosy a picture – regional opportunities for mobility exist that are independent of the globally ranked 'power of passports'.

The term 'regional integration' is used to refer to the voluntary and long-term cooperation between states in a region, with the aim of deeper economic integration and political collaboration. Sometimes this extends to the establishment of supranational institutions and communitization. For many states, regionalization is an important intermediate level between the model of the nation-state and globalization, since the formation of regional economic zones allows them to benefit from the advantages of cross-border trade and movement of capital, without necessarily opting for complete and unmitigated integration into the world market. Regional integration is sometimes seen as an integral component (or subset) of globalization, by analogy with a Russian matryoshka doll. At other times, however, the dominant view is that regional integration projects are attempts to preserve the agency of nation-states in conditions of globalization: alliances with other countries are the only way to make the pressure of the world market manageable.

From the perspective of the border, the interesting thing about these regional integration processes is that they create new areas of circulation. Since regional integration is often focused on the establishment of common markets and the intensification of economic exchange, borders are seen as inhibiting the market. Many regional integration initiatives go beyond freedom of movement for goods and services and also aim to give the citizens of member states greater opportunities for mobility.[8] This ranges from improving mobility rights for workers to granting full rights of residence and establishment. Thus, integration involves the opening of the member states to each other, simplifying movement between them, but at the same time it can lead to a restructuring of external relations. This regionalization can be described as 'macroterritorialization': the formation of territorial areas with independent mobility regimes, made up of several countries.

One of the first of these multilateral collaborations, aimed at creating a single open mobility area, was the Nordic Passport Union (NPU), established in 1954 by Denmark, Finland, Sweden, Norway and Iceland, within the framework of the Nordic Council. The objective at the time was greater permeability of the national borders between these countries. Citizens could travel from one country to another without a visa, and were allowed to reside and establish themselves without a residence or work permit. A passport was no longer needed, and today not even a proof of identity is legally required. Passport checks at the internal borders were also abolished for citizens of non-member states, so free, unimpeded mobility became possible for them too. The Schengen area, created a few decades later, was not dissimilar to this model: it distinguished between internal and external borders, removed internal border controls, and institutionalized the right to freedom of movement in order to create a 'mobile Europe'.⁹

Attempts at regional integration are found not only in Europe, but in many regions of the world, for example in Africa (ECOWAS – Economic Community of West African States), South America (Mercosur – Mercado Común del Sur) and Asia (ASEAN – Association of Southeast Asian Nations). In total, depending on one's method of counting, there are twenty to thirty such unions, but with very different ambitions and degrees of integration. In South America, the creation of Mercosur – consisting of Argentina, Brazil, Paraguay, Uruguay and Venezuela – established a common internal market with free movement of capital, goods, services and people. Free movement of workers was a declared goal of the group's efforts at integration right from the start, and in 2002 this resulted in an agreement on freedom of movement and freedom of establishment in the Mercosur states and associated countries. The members of ECOWAS signed a joint protocol in 1979 agreeing to abolish entry visas and other entry permits for 'community citizens', though there are still national regulations on immigration and border control. In 2000, a unified ECOWAS passport was issued to facilitate mobility within the region, and roadblocks and checkpoints were dismantled. In ASEAN, the main objective is to create a free-trade zone; the free movement of people lags behind and is limited to easier access to visas and work permits for skilled workers and specific occupational groups.

The EU's Schengen area and the associated EU regulations – described as the largest free travel zone in the world – currently constitute the most advanced form of macroterritorialization. The deinstitutionalization of the internal borders is aimed at creating an integrated economic and social area, which includes a common mobility area. The 'four freedoms' that make up the core of the integration programme – the free movement of goods, capital, services and people – work on the principle that barriers hindering cross-border movement should be dismantled, whether they be legal, tariff-related or physical. Access to national territories was previously regulated by individual states, using credit and capital controls, regulations on residence and work permits, and customs duties. Now, however, the member states have very little scope to restrict entry and exit or cross-border transactions. Citizens of the union have the right to move freely within the EU, to settle, or to accept a job. In some areas, rights to freedom of movement have also been extended to people from non-EU countries with a permanent right of residence.

Between the Schengen countries, all border controls have been abolished and all checkpoints dismantled. Schengen, a small town in Luxembourg, has become the emblematic term for the disappearance of border queues and boom barriers, and for the idea of unimpeded (and undisturbed) travel. Travellers passing through 'Schengen' no longer encounter any controlled borders, and may not even notice whether and when they have crossed a border. At airports, checks are only carried out on incoming travellers from countries that do not belong to the Schengen group. However, temporary controls are allowed for exceptional situations (where security is at stake or a particular threat is imminent). In the last several years such temporary controls have been used more and more frequently, not least because of the increasingly pressing issue of migration and, most recently, the Covid-19 pandemic.[10] Interestingly, it is mainly the countries in Northern and Western Europe that make use of this instrument.[11]

Macroterritorialization is not just focused on the interior, it can also have external effects. In fact, the two things are interconnected, as the example of the EU shows. Under the Schengen Agreement, border control functions have been combined and displaced to the common external borders, while fixed border controls in the interior have been eliminated (checkpoints and border huts dismantled, border guards withdrawn).[12] Here, internal opening and external border security are interrelated: the lowering or removal of internal borders is conditional on adequate protection and control of the external borders (which are now common to the whole union) to ensure that individual member states need not fear any negative consequences.[13] We can even say that the external borders have been 'upgraded' to the same extent that borders between member states have been dismantled. Border functions that were previously the remit of the individual states have been delegated to the (now common) external border, imposing particular political and social costs on countries at the outer edges. Countries with a border that coincides with the external border of the EU/Schengen area have had to reorganize their border relations with countries outside the Schengen area. For example, local cross-border trade and movement have had to be stopped, and long-established relationships with non-EU neighbours have been hampered or even rendered impossible by the upgrading of the border. The EU's border states have committed to supplying 'forces' in 'sufficient numbers' to monitor the external borders. Regular checks are carried out to ensure that the conditions linked to the removal of controls at the internal borders, that is, the control and surveillance of the external borders, are being met. Greece, for example, joined the Schengen Agreement in 1992, but the agreement was not implemented there for several years because the Schengen Executive Committee expressed security concerns about entry procedures at Greek seaports and airports. Thus, the countries on the outskirts are mandated to act as guards for the entire Schengen zone. In the words of Ursula von der Leyen, currently President of the EU Commission, Greece has become Europe's 'shield' in recent years.[14] This has led to severe distortions in matters of asylum and subsidiary protection, since the Dublin procedure stipulates that asylum applications should be processed in the country where the refugee first enters the EU. This provision disadvantages the countries at the EU's external borders, making them the stopping point and often the end point for refugees on their way to the core countries of the EU.

The EU has supported this hardening of the outer borders by establishing an integrated border management fund and building up the European border protection agency Frontex (now officially called the European Border and Coast Guard Agency). Border fences and surveillance systems have been financed and set up, Frontex officials are deployed at the external borders, and there is continuous coordination of border-related measures. Frontex currently numbers around 1,000 staff, but is expected to grow to 10,000 by 2027. At the same time, its powers of intervention have been gradually expanded: in situations of acute danger, the agency can even send guards to a member state against the will of that state if the majority of other members support this.

Another aspect of the hardening of the border is the recording, storage and exchange of personal data by means of the Schengen Information System (SIS). At the same time, various agencies throughout Europe have been given greater access to this data: Europol, Eurojust and Frontex are all entitled to access the system. The Prüm Convention, mentioned in the previous chapter, allows DNA information and biometric data to be accessed and exchanged across national borders. Like goods and capital, data and personal information now circulate across borders with little hindrance.[15] These systems, in combination with other databases such as the fingerprint database Eurodac and the Visa Information System (VIS), are being used to develop a common identity repository. Data on 'high-risk' individuals provided by other countries such as the US is also fed into the system. In future, the plan is to store fingerprints and personal data recorded at the external borders as standard practice. A concrete step planned for the near future is an 'entry/exit system', which will record data from all third-country nationals when they enter the Schengen area (name, date of birth, fingerprints, photo), thus creating a comprehensive register of third-country nationals. This shows how 'smart borders' can become an essential component of a regional integration project.

In its external relations, Schengen has become a relatively closed and unified mobility area. Travellers from more than 100 countries – no less than 80 per cent of the world's population excluding the EU – need a visa to enter the Schengen area. Visa waivers apply to the usual suspects, those we have already identified as having mobility privileges (mainly the citizens of rich democracies, but also of other wealthy states). The Schengen visa for short-term stays of up to ninety days is valid for the entire Schengen zone, regardless of which embassy or consulate issues the visa; holders of this visa can move freely within the Schengen area. In other words, the individual member states have given up their claim to national decision-making. The Schengen process also involves common standards for issuing visas, and a uniform list of third countries with visa exemptions. Even if there are still some idiosyncrasies in the administrative process, it should no longer make any difference which Schengen country one applies to for a visa: in theory, there should be no opportunity for 'visa shopping' and no scope to exploit more liberal decision-making practices.

The former president of Ukraine, Leonid Kuchma, once complained that the Schengen visa has replaced the Iron Curtain, and that there was now a 'paper curtain' – more humane, perhaps, but no less difficult to overcome. The comparison may sound inappropriate, and yet, a few years ago it was normal to see queues in front of the German embassy in Kyiv, and Ukrainians wishing to enter the EU faced enormous difficulties. There was great jubilation when, after years of negotiations and political pressure, travel rules were relaxed and Ukrainian citizens were able to enter the EU without a visa. When visa-free tourist travel was announced for citizens of Western Balkan countries such as Serbia, people threw parties and fired rockets into the air, delighted to see the end of what had often been perceived as a bureaucratic labyrinth. In Kosovo, the last country in the Balkans whose citizens need a visa for tourist travel to the EU, the experience of applying for a visa is often Kafkaesque. The subject has even inspired a comedy show, *Schengen Visa*.

Although the EU/Schengen area can be regarded as unique in terms of the creation of a unified mobility area, it is not the only regional integration project focusing on the facilitation of internal mobility, as mentioned above. Worldwide, there are more than two dozen regional organizations or agreements with a stated commitment to facilitating the mobility of people.[16] Their founding documents often mention, at least as a long-term goal, unrestricted freedom of movement, and sometimes also freedom of establishment. The starting point is usually an interest in economic integration, and the basic principle is that of 'free movement of persons, goods, capital and services', since the combination of these four freedoms is seen as central for the development of a common market. Freedom of movement within these regional organizations is therefore conceived of not in abstract normative terms, but mainly in economic and functional terms. This is why the emphasis is often on specific groups such as skilled workers, service providers, business people or seasonal workers. Overall, however, the degree of internal integration (and internal openness) varies considerably: some projects have stalled on the way to a customs union; in others, conflicts between important member states have brought the dynamic of integration to a standstill. Nonetheless, a survey of these zones of regional integration shows that the role of macroterritorial border formation in the structuring of mobility should not be underestimated.[17]

We will return to the central issue of visa policies to illustrate this. Projects of regional integration generally make use of a wide range of visa-related measures, such as the suspension of visa requirements for local border traffic, the granting of permanent or long-term visas, or the facilitation of travel for groups of workers and business people. In many regional organizations, internal visa requirements have been removed. Like the EU, the Eurasian Economic Community (EAEU) has made free travel possible throughout its territory, so citizens of the member states can move freely with their identity document. The situation is similar – with restrictions – in the Commonwealth of Independent States (CIS) and the Gulf Cooperation Council (GCC).

Sometimes the right of establishment is also granted, and citizens of other countries are given equal legal status. Mercosur has introduced extensive visa waivers, and people from the member states can even visit other countries in the region with just their ID card. The Andean Community (CAN: Comunidad Andina de Naciones) has also facilitated mobility; in 2001 it even introduced its own passport, which is intended to replace national passports. Like the EU, the Andean Community and Mercosur have installed priority counters for their own citizens at airports. In contrast, the North American Free Trade Agreement (NAFTA) shows a much lower level of internal openness, due to the hesitancy of the US.

It is not possible to enumerate all the mobility policies associated with regional integration processes here, nor can we trace their actual implementation. Agreements on opening, as found in treaties and protocols, are not always ratified by all states. Sometimes only lip service is paid to them, because national territorial interests ultimately prevail. Nonetheless, we have strong evidence of the reorganization of mobility rights in the framework of regional integration:[18] in Figure 4, the examples of the EU, ECOWAS and ASEAN serve to document how visa-free travel in different regional organizations has changed over time, in terms of internal and external relations. The measurement is based on an index of visa restrictiveness. The cases examined show a development towards internal openness, while the degree of closure towards external countries remains surprisingly stable in the forty-year window observed (even though this coincides with the period of globalization). The globalization of opening seems to be quite regional in scope.

In our own research on regional visa policies, we empirically investigated the question of internal opening and external closure or unification for a total of eight

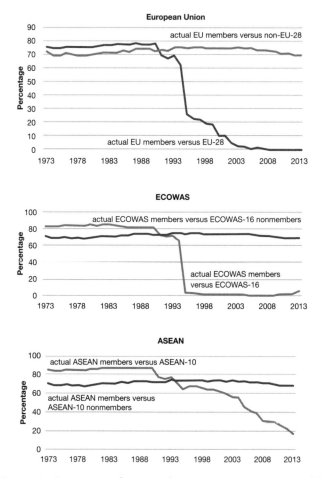

Figure 4: Openness of regional organizations, measured by visa restrictiveness

Note: DEMIG Visa Data. The graphs show a 'visa restrictiveness index', which calculates the proportion of countries that need a visa for entry. A distinction is made between member states and non-member states. On each graph, one line shows visa requirements towards member states (showing a downward trend in each case) and the other shows visa requirements towards non-members (little to no change).

Source: Mathias Czaika, Hein de Haas and María Villares-Varela, 'The Global Evolution of Travel Visa Regimes', *Population and Development Review*, 44/3 (2018), p. 613.

regionalization projects, based on their visa relations.[19] Our findings were very clear: in most cases (as in the above-mentioned examples), internal openness has increased substantially over time. The countries involved have made their borders more permeable for each other, gradually removing visa requirements. Internal tourist travel is completely visa-free not only in the EU, but also in the East African Community (EAC) and ECOWAS. Mercosur is almost at the same level; and the Southern African Development Community (SADC) also shows signs of moving (albeit slowly) towards greater openness. Our data makes it clear that the lowering of barriers to mobility and the facilitation of internal border crossings are inherent in these processes of regionalization, and are a core element of integration projects.

According to our study, however, a dynamic of opening only develops if the economic level within these communities is balanced, if the differences between the political systems remain limited, and if there are no deep conflicts between the member countries. Major internal economic disparities or political tensions impede integration and opening, because some of the countries involved fear negative spill-over effects. The case of South Africa is instructive in this context. SADC has had a 'Draft Protocol on the Facilitation of Movement of Persons' since 2005, but South Africa has delayed its implementation because, as the wealthiest country in the community, it is afraid of uncontrolled immigration and is attempting to defend itself with tighter border controls. It has even invested in fences and barriers at its borders with poorer neighbours, thus joining the ranks of the fortified states. As in the case of the EU, we also see numerous examples of regional integration, where the opening of the internal area is accompanied by a greater coherence in external relations, and a harmonization of the visa waivers accorded to third countries.

Compared to Schengen, other regional organizations show fewer signs of a real macroterritorial hardening of external borders. Here too, however, we can see that greater internal openness leads to increased pressure to at least harmonize external border relations. Commentators have repeatedly highlighted the nexus between internal liberalization and opening of borders, on the one hand, and, on the other, joint governance and hardening of external borders.[20] When it comes to customs and import regulations and the movement of goods, capital and services, common rules are both a precondition and a direct consequence of the establishment of an internal market. In the case of free movement of people, this pressure also exists, but the obstacles to communitization are much higher here – and these efforts are often thwarted by national self-interest. Nonetheless, there are indications that the regional organizations outside Europe are also working on common standards of control, be it by developing common or mutually recognized travel documents, sharing information, creating databases with extended rights of access, or training border guards. Another area of activity is the development of a joint framework for managing and regulating migration and mobility into the economic zone in question. If these different integration projects continue along the path to full internal freedom of movement and the removal of border controls between the member states, then they will also move towards a common border policy. The establishment of common visa policies (or the introduction of visas valid in multiple states), the upgrading of the common external border, and the delegation of control functions are already very much part of the debate.[21]

Overall, the picture outlined here shows that questions of borders and mobility cannot be fully understood if we only look at the global hierarchy of states and at the obvious North–South divide. These are unquestionably an essential structural feature of globalization, but the often-overlooked regional level between nation-state and world society has its own distinctive dynamic of development. Clearly, we are seeing the emergence of extended regional areas of circulation, which no longer coincide with the container spaces of the nation-state model. With their regional scale, they cut across the global hierarchy of mobility described above, and can give people opportunities for mobility within their specific contexts. This points to a multipolar rather than a merely bipolar world order. At the same time, the macroterritorial context confirms what we have seen before: that the globalization of opening, understood as a politics of integration focused on the freedom of movement, can also be accompanied by closures.

8

Extraterritorializing Control: The Expansion of the Border Zone

In the German political debate, it has become commonplace to say that the country's security must be defended in the Hindu Kush, a mountain range in Central Asia. Similarly, any politician responsible for migration issues may tell you that the southern border of Germany does not lie between Germany and Switzerland or Germany and Austria, but in the Mediterranean or North Africa, or actually even further south, in sub-Saharan Africa. This is where the outposts of European/German border policies are to be found, policies aimed at containing and controlling the influx of migrants from Africa. Niger, one of the world's poorest countries and more than 5,000 kilometres from Berlin, is regarded as the key transit hub for irregular migration from southern and western Africa, which is why the country has attracted the interest of Brussels and Berlin. For some years, the executive has been trying to prevent groups of people from heading north through the Sahara by coercing neighbouring states into cooperation and making them part of European border and migration management. Borders that had previously received little attention, informal borders crossed daily by traders, cattle breeders and farmers, have gradually become the furthest outposts of European border policy. In response to pressure from the EU, Niger passed a law against people smuggling in 2015. For many years, the EU has supported the training and development of border personnel to stop refugees who are heading for Libya, and has promised the government financial assistance if it turns its border into a barrier for people in transit. Water sources are now guarded in order to make the journey through the desert difficult – and potentially deadly. In Agadez, the largest city and the most important place of transit in the centre of the country, police checks aimed at arresting potential migrants are now a common sight.

The example of Niger is representative of a wider trend: the externalization, displacement and spatial diffusion of border controls. The border of control, especially that of countries in the Global North, has moved away from the borderline. To accurately depict the significance of this development, we have to make a small but important analytical distinction: between the actual territorial course of the border (border I) and the border in its function of exerting territorial control (border II). Border I, the border represented on the map, is fixed and unchanging. Border II, the border of control, can shift spatially and change location. Border II can be found wherever mobility is monitored, wherever state agencies intervene in people's spatial movements, wherever border areas of restricted movement are created, wherever new border zones are formed. For the French philosopher Étienne Balibar, the decoupling of border control from a fixed location is a key characteristic, perhaps the decisive feature of new border formations, because it causes a fundamental shift in the relationship between the territory and the border.[1] A contemporary understanding of borders, according to Balibar, must concentrate not on a specific place – the territorial border – but on the exercise of selective control and the prevention of migration and mobility, wherever this happens. Instead of focusing on the movement of mobile people across borders, the analytical gaze must consider the movement of borders towards mobile people.[2] Here the binary, territorial understanding of borders – this side and that side, inside and outside – is inevitably overturned. We are no longer dealing with borders between states, but with 'plurilocal' borders, which can have very different spatial relationships to the territory. This trend towards the displacement of control has been discussed and framed in various terms – for example, as the spatial flexibilization of border controls,[3] extraterritorialization,[4] 'pushing the border out', or 'shifting borders'.[5]

New, spatially flexible control arrangements can be understood as functional equivalents and supplements to forms of selectivity that were previously implemented at the fixed border. Here, control can be made both more intensive and more extensive, and can ultimately achieve more than what was and is customary at the land border. The 'new border' is not only movable, shifting away from territorial entry points; another defining feature is that it is not aimed at all mobile people, it is not a border for everybody. Rather, the delocalized and relocalized border exerts control in a highly selective way and focuses only on certain groups, which become the targets of rigid practices of control. The extraterritorialized border therefore develops a new, narrower definition of the circle of people who are to be targeted by the border. Instead of sending everyone through a checkpoint, which functions as an entry portal, it acts – metaphorically speaking – as a roaming guard dog, sounding the alarm whenever suspect individuals approach its property.

A shift in the location of border control can essentially go in two directions: inwards or outwards. In the latter case, it is extraterritorialization. In some respects, the inner borders of control are not new (think 'immigration police'), so we will only mention them briefly here. It should be noted, however, that they (like the outer borders) have gained importance and undergone a change in form. Many countries have seen a systematic expansion in the checks carried out by the police and other government agencies to enforce regulations relating to residence and registration. They target people who have lost their right of residence and are to be 'repatriated', 'illegal' workers and visa overstayers. Entry/exit database systems, which are currently under development, register travellers as they enter a territory and inform the authorities automatically if the permitted stay has been exceeded. The state's established methods of controlling mobility also include tracking and tracing, mandatory registration, the criminalization of irregular migration and unauthorized residence, and checks carried out in crime hotspots without specific grounds for suspicion.[6] When the Schengen area was created, regular checks at the internal borders were suspended and border facilities were dismantled, but the control zone was expanded into the interior of the territory to compensate. Instead of fixed checkpoints, there are now mobile border controls, which can be carried out near the border (up to thirty kilometres away from it), but also in transport hubs such as motorway services and railway stations. So, although the border initially seemed to have disappeared, it has returned in a different form. The staff who previously worked at the border now conduct checks elsewhere and with different criteria, which focus on suspicion and are in many ways similar to police investigations. Alongside these government activities, a kind of 'everyday bordering'[7] takes place: employers, transport companies, landlords or ordinary citizens are enlisted to perform certain control functions, such as examining residence permits and supporting documents and complying with registration requirements. For example, there are several countries where shop or restaurant owners who want to employ people must first check the legal status of the applicants and inform the authorities if there are any irregularities. In some border areas there are even self-authorized citizen patrols, who behave as if they were border police with a mandate to search for irregular migrants. (In 2016, citizen patrols in Bulgaria actually went out hunting for refugees.) There is also a growing commercial security industry, with paramilitary organizational structures and trained personnel, which is taking over surveillance and control functions. Here, some of what were once sovereign functions of the state are being delegated to private actors.

Moving border II outwards is a challenging undertaking, but one that security agencies see as effective and therefore attractive. States extend their interventions beyond their own territory: control becomes an extra-territorial matter, and a versatile new border, adaptable to changing circumstances, is created outside the line of demarcation. Border control can be externalized unilaterally, but there has also been an intensification of international or multilateral cooperation between states in the organization of new borders, for example in the exchange of information, the logistics of control and cooperation on the level of security services. Structures reflecting internationalized border policies are also emerging in the context of international organizations such as the International Organization for Migration (IOM), the United Nations High Commissioner for Refugees (UNHCR) and the International Labour Organization (ILO). These are mainly focused on the 'management of migration'.

Travellers and migrants often encounter the externalized border before they even leave their country of origin, but the new border also encompasses transit routes and modes of transport. This means that checkpoints at the territorial border of the destination country are, at most, the final control post before entry. In her study on 'Border Controls Beyond National Territories', one of my former doctoral students, Lena Laube, systematically traced this development and produced an overview of the measures and instruments of externalized control.[8] It shows the whole spectrum of remote management and control of mobility, encompassing tourists, business travellers, labour migrants and refugees. These forms of externalized control have mainly been developed by liberal Western states. Canada, the EU, Australia and the US in particular have flexibilized and expanded control to such an extent that the barrier effect of borders often begins thousands of kilometres away from their territory. Movable borders of control aim to prevent 'unwelcome' travellers from leaving, transiting or arriving.[9] This programme of 'pushing the border out' is usually combined with the criminalization of humanitarian and other types of migration, sometimes referred to as 'crimmigration'.[10] This leads to a framing of migration that is less about the protection of human rights and vulnerable groups, and more about emphasizing aspects of crime and human trafficking, to stress the legitimacy of the new restrictions on mobility.[11]

So what are the main instruments of the extraterritorialization of control? It is possible to ask (following Lena Laube) both where the control takes place and who exerts it. For the 'where', we can differentiate between the country of origin, the transit route and the place of arrival (see Figure 5). The 'who' includes the deployment of national officials abroad and the delegation of control functions to third parties, such as private companies or other countries (as in Niger). Such collaborations with countries of origin and transit are generally not voluntary, nor are they agreements between equals; often they are achieved coercively with a mixture of incentives and sanctions. A citizen

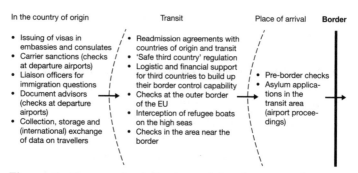

Figure 5: Extraterritorialization of border control: externalized sites of control

Source: Based on a table in Lena Laube, *Grenzkontrollen jenseits nationaler Territorien: Die Steuerung globaler Mobilität durch liberale Staaten*, Frankfurt am Main: Campus, 2013, p. 151.

from the Global South wishing to travel north will first encounter the outposts of national administrations in consular offices, which issue visas and thus authorize both travel to and entry into a destination country (though a separate decision is still made at the actual border crossing). Although these officials serving in the field are obliged to follow a visa codex, they still have considerable discretion, as the different rejection rates show.[12] This remote control over the granting of visas plays a major role in the management of mobility, as we saw in Chapter 5 on filtering borders.

The next step is to integrate transport companies into the control system, by prohibiting them from transporting people who do not have a valid travel document. Historically, the imposition of sanctions on carriers is not new, but there has been a sharp increase in the penalties for rule violations, which are understood as aiding and abetting illegal border crossings. Carriers are also obliged to bear the costs of returning people without an entry or residence permit. As a consequence, airlines and bus companies closely examine passports and visas, indirectly providing control services to the state. At airports, they are supported and supervised by 'liaison officers' or 'document advisers'. Passenger processing measures become *de facto* border controls. This is also shown by the fact that airlines (e.g., in the US and Europe) are obliged to collect a substantial quantity of passenger data in advance and to share it with the authorities in the destination countries. This pre-screening and the sharing of passenger data prior to travel extend the control of state agencies both temporally and spatially. For example, databases can be consulted and risk assessments undertaken hours before travellers actually enter the country, allowing a more intense focus on 'problem cases' immediately after arrival. This involves a close and data-sensitive integration of control activities by private companies and the state. An especially problematic aspect of this approach is that it could prevent victims of political persecution from leaving their home country: it is not really possible to submit an asylum application to airport personnel.[13] Even before the actual border crossing, international airports in many destination countries contain transit zones with a special legal status, where fast-track asylum procedures are carried out. The practice of defining such zones as extraterritorial, even though they are located in a particular state territory, makes it possible to send people back to their country of origin or transit immediately if their asylum application is rejected. In general, then, the attempt to reach a destination country has become an obstacle course with an uncertain outcome for migrants and 'undesirable' travellers. This applies particularly to those seeking humanitarian protection.

As mentioned above, enlisting other states to secure one's own borders is a key tool in the extraterritorialization of control. Questions of power and financial incentives play a major part in persuading other countries to shut down access routes and to take back migrants or prevent them from continuing their journey.[14] For these countries, this often requires intensification and tightening of their own border policing measures, which must now be organized so as to serve the defensive interests of a potential destination country or region. Whole countries or areas can thus be converted into the border zones of other, often very remote, countries. For years, the US has attempted to integrate Mexico and other Central American countries into its border policies, so that people who leave their homes because of poverty and natural disasters can be kept away from the US border. As an example, the threat of customs duties on Mexican exports to the US motivated Mexico to reinforce its southern border. The EU has often used the prospect of visa waivers to encourage neighbouring states and those in the 'periphery' to take on border control functions.[15] These are moves towards openness at the expense of third parties: such states are only granted visa-free travel if they are prepared to reduce the mobility of people from other countries. Here opening (for oneself) and closing (for others) go hand in hand.

The 'safe third-country' regulation is another part of the strategy of externalization. The principle of non-refoulement, enshrined in international law, states that people may not be sent back to countries where they are threatened by torture or human rights violations. This limits the options for refusing entry at the border to a person who is persecuted or in need of protection. However, states circumvent these duties of protection by defining other countries as safe. They then send asylum-seekers who have entered via a so-called safe third country back to that country, claiming that it is responsible for granting asylum. Countries can shut off access via land both *de jure* and *de facto* as long as they are surrounded by safe third countries. It is as if an island state were to say that people were only permitted to enter via the overland route. The excessive use of this classification and the political battle over what can be defined as a 'safe third country' make it clear that the territorial displacement of responsibilities and rights of protection and the creation of special zones and waiting areas are powerful tools for limiting humanitarian migration. Australia, for example, relies on territorial 'offshoring' solutions, and has built camps on the South Pacific islands of Nauru und Manus (though the Manus Regional Processing Centre has now been closed and replaced by three new accommodation centres). Refugees intercepted at sea are brought to these camps so that their asylum applications can be examined far away from Australian territory (though a positive outcome does not mean that they are allowed to enter Australia – far from it!).

There has also been a massive proliferation of readmission agreements: many countries in the Global South have agreed to take back 'undesirable' or 'illegal' immigrants in return for financial aid or the easing of travel restrictions. Europe has developed a dense and rapidly growing network of such agreements. We must distinguish here between contracts that only oblige countries to take back their own citizens, and those aimed at returning anyone who has crossed their territory in transit.[16] In the 1970s only a handful of these agreements existed; today, they form a tightly woven web around the globe. In the mid-1980s the EU-12 had signed just thirty-three such agreements; today, the EU-27 have more than 300 in place.[17] The cooperation agreement between the EU and Turkey in March 2016, commonly known as the 'refugee deal', was ultimately an agreement of this type, designed to limit immigration into Europe: the European states paid money so that Turkey would keep or readmit the refugees. To encourage Turkey to support the EU's border security interests, they also set a timetable for visa liberalization for Turkish citizens, and promised to resume accession talks.

For the EU, the externalization of border controls and the development of the border protection agency, Frontex, are further important steps towards the extra-territorialization of control, as discussed in Chapter 7 on macroterritorialization. In that chapter I also pointed out that control at the outer border of the EU has been concentrated and intensified to compensate for the dismantling of border controls between the Schengen countries. As a result, countries like Greece and Italy now take on control functions on behalf of all the other member states. They become, often involuntarily, the bouncers guarding the doors of the house of Europe (or 'fortress Europe', depending on one's perspective). The states bordering the Mediterranean secure Europe's sea border, with support from Frontex and personnel and technology from other member states – though often the legal situation is unclear and their actions conflict with humanitarian values. These operations on the water and off the coast of Africa serve to intercept and return migrants before they reach European soil, to prevent them from accessing the legal systems of protection. This border regime has not only generated images of overcrowded and foundering rubber dinghies and exhausted helpers from civilian sea rescue organizations; it is also responsible for the deaths of many people who have drowned trying to reach Europe.

Tensions may also arise, however, between extra-territorialization and macroterritorialization, if the outsourcing of control undermines regional efforts to achieve greater openness. Let us return to the example of Niger – though we could also mention Mali, Nigeria or Senegal. Niger is a member of ECOWAS, which is committed to the free movement of people and sees this as one of its integration goals. This goal has been partly achieved: citizens of member states have the right to travel in and out of the other states without a visa, and to stay in another country for work purposes. Yet thanks to the extraterritorialization of EU border control to Niger, and the integration of this country into the EU's attempts to control migration (in a programme officially called the 'Migration Partnership Framework'), citizens of other ECOWAS states have once again become the targets of state control – even though the ECOWAS protocol states that they should be able to move freely. For example, if local carriers transport people without valid papers from other ECOWAS states, this is now – after pressure from the EU – classed as people smuggling, and penalized. New border posts are being established, more checks are being carried out inside the country, and at the same time there has been a drive for more biometric data collection and increased technologization of border controls. As a result, some people are already calling Niger the 'immigration agency of Europe'.[18] The EU supports such measures directly, but also links development aid with expectations of border reinforcement – the deal is 'money against migration'.[19] At the same time, the EU ostensibly encourages the African countries to press on with integration, and supports freedom of movement within ECOWAS. Here there is an inevitable clash between the objective of global management of irregular migration and the free movement regulations within a regional economic community.

This externalization of borders can be seen simply as the extension of previous fixed border controls, yet it has much more far-reaching legal, political and social implications. If states increasingly resort to extraterritorial methods in their efforts to gain territorial control, they are intervening in spaces and mobility in the territories of other countries. Legal scholar Ayelet Shachar has lucidly argued that our legal system has a strong territorial component: extraterritorialization severs the link between control and access to rights, and systematically keeps the subjects of control at a distance.[20] The externalization of control leads to a legal vacuum, since many rights to protection can only be claimed after entry into a territory. This 'remote control' creates legally precarious zones, where the paradigm of security trumps that of protection. Furthermore, extraterritorial border control often operates away from the public eye, as an invisible force working to securitize mobility and migration.[21] This gap between the exercise of control and legal protection becomes clearest when we consider asylum: the prerequisite for a successful asylum application is arrival in the territory of a country with a reliable right to claim asylum. But if such a country surrounds itself with supposedly 'safe third countries', and prohibits carriers from transporting people without the necessary visas or residence permits, then no asylum application can be lodged. So countries that extend the long arm of control need not fear any unwanted migration.

Shachar argues that this system privileges those groups who – for whatever reasons – have made it to a territory and are able to claim rights to protection there (she talks about the 'overrated premium of territorial arrival').[22] She believes that this is inherently unjust, and creates the wrong incentives. On this basis, Shachar makes clear that if a state's border controls move, then established rights to claim protection from that state should move with them. This would mean subjecting extraterritorial control to legal parameters much more than is currently the case, ideally even imposing a unified legal framework identical to that valid within the territory. State actors or those acting on their behalf would then take their legal obligations with them, as it were, to the site of control. The second part of Shachar's recommendations is to loosen the connection between access to a particular territory and access to rights, so that 'touching the ground' is no longer the main criterion for legal protection. States should be obliged to provide help (e.g., to accept contingents of refugees) even if refugees have not yet left their own country. The proposal to establish asylum centres in North Africa, repeatedly discussed in the EU, would be an example of such an approach. It is extremely challenging, however, to extend legal procedures beyond one's own territory if the usual standards are to be applied: questions of legal assistance, the right to appeal decisions and the mobilization of civil society must all be taken into account.

This call for congruence between legal responsibility and (externalized) border control is both necessary and normatively convincing, yet it seems most unlikely that it will actually be implemented as policy. The inclusion of human rights and international refugee law in national constitutions has strengthened the individual as a legal subject in relation to state authorities. National laws based on international obligations (e.g., on questions of displacement, asylum and family reunification) limit the nation-state's scope to decide – at its sole discretion – who is allowed to enter its territory.[23] These 'shifting borders' are essentially a reaction to the challenge faced by states: that of living up to their own liberal ethos and meeting the obligations this entails, while pursuing their interest in limiting and controlling migration and mobility at their own discretion. The extraterritorialization of border control is not motivated solely by questions of greater efficacy; a key driver is the desire of (in particular) liberal states to escape their own self-imposed normative commitments. The recurring EU debate about offshore asylum centres encapsulates the primary motive of the member states: to prevent refugees from even leaving their own countries. The idea is that asylum applications will be examined remotely rather than in the destination country, to keep those seeking protection at a distance. This would mean that states could use the legally underregulated sites of control outside the border to creatively circumvent their own legal obligations. This would be an attempt to create scope for illiberality in order to cope with the challenges that globalization creates for migration policy. The questionable pushbacks carried out in the Mediterranean by the EU border protection agency Frontex, forcing refugee boats back into international waters, are a revealing indication of how eager the EU and related organizations are to prevent migration, and how willing they are to set aside their own legal obligations.

Given that legal responsibility is an impediment to their ambitions for control, then, why would states have any interest in spatially expanding it? After all, extraterritorialization is a response to the constraints that countries often face at their own borders. The price of such an expansion of legal responsibility would be a narrowing of their options for management and decision-making. In light of migration pressures and reservations about humanitarian obligations within the domestic political sphere, it is highly doubtful whether governments will be willing to pay this price. By externalizing control, states give themselves scope for defence and deterrence which they would not have within the framework of their liberal order. The externalization of the border is seen as a proven and promising method of migration management in conditions of globalization. Here the modus of closure is not to withdraw, snail-like, into the protective shell of the nation-state, but to expand beyond the national territory. The state in its role as border guard does not retreat into a defensive position of territorial containment, but extends its reach, and – in the national interest – becomes a globalized actor, embedded in international contexts.

9

Globalized Borders

How do borders operate in the twenty-first century? That question was the starting point for this book, a small book with a large subject, perhaps too large a subject. If we think back to the academic and public debates from the turn of the century, we find an almost unfettered optimism about globalization. It seemed there was only one possible vision for the future: a transition from a world of nation-states to a globally connected world community, where goods, information, capital and people would move freely across borders. The doctrine was not new. It had its origins in a view prevalent (in the Western world) since the Second World War: that a system of states shaped by trade and economic openness would be more peaceful and would benefit everyone. In these narratives, the 'world without borders' was perhaps not quite within reach, but was not implausible as a long-term development. From the perspective of a world of relatively closed nation-states, processes of debordering, deterritorialization and delocalization could be observed in nearly all areas. These suggested, at least indirectly, that borders and their function as 'interrupters of interdependence' and 'dividers of space' – once so important – were now becoming weaker and more irrelevant. In any case, the gradual obsolescence of the border and the increasing porosity of the container state were always implicitly envisaged.

Amid all this movement, the question of cross-border mobility of people had a special status, yet many took it for granted that interconnectedness in the areas of the economy, culture, politics, etc. would inevitably lead to greater freedom of movement for people – and therefore more movement. And, in fact, there has never, in the history of humanity, been such a strong social consolidation, such an intensification of connectivity across regions, continents and national borders. Never have we been so closely interconnected, and never has the cross-border mobility of people been so great. In social relations, work contexts and family life, globalization has led hundreds of millions of people out of the container of the nation-state, and has made the crossing of borders a widely shared experience. It has created a world in movement, a world of interactions.

There is no denying that globalization has substantially weakened the movement-inhibiting effect of borders, and has accelerated processes of opening. But the idea of a literally 'borderless' globalization is a chimera. Contrary to our everyday intuition, globalization also creates and reinforces borders – there is a globalization of closure. Yet if our understanding of borders is limited to walls, barbed wire and fortifications, then we will overlook a large proportion of today's diversified forms of borders and control. Instead of talking about 'vanishing borders',[1] it becomes clear on closer inspection that it is more appropriate to think in terms of a reinvention, hardening and securitization of borders in conditions of globalization – not to mention the fact that walled borders have also grown in number and length. Even in the first phase of globalization at the end of the nineteenth century, border infrastructures were developed, new technologies of registration and control were implemented and laws regarding travel and residence were codified. Similar processes seem to be underway today, though the sorting function of the border has now become increasingly prominent. Of course, borders have always been selective, but rarely in the course of history has the coding of every single traveller as desirable or undesirable, high risk or low risk, been carried out with such thoroughness.

Today, the border is no longer a national matter, limited to the national territory; it is a complex, internationalized sorting machine, an ensemble of legal regulations, agencies of control, the utilization of other countries, data and technology. This spatial expansion of the reach of the border, beyond the national sphere, is part of the globalization of closure. The phenomenon emerging here is what Saskia Sassen has called the 'paradox of the national':[2] through these forms of 'remote control',[3] the nation-state itself is involved in the constitution of global conditions, and this involvement reflects its identifiable interests of territorial closure, management of mobility and control. The global begins in and leads back to the national. This reveals both functional and spatial aspects of the globalization of closure – functional, in that selective closure or the reinforcement of the filtering function is inherent in opening, and is intensified by it; spatial, in that the instruments of control, closure and selectivity themselves expand and become global. The territorial state now operates globally and transnationally; even in the prevention and control of border crossing, it is a powerful agent of globalization.

The border in the twenty-first century is visible and invisible, geographically fixed and flexible, physical and virtual, permanent and occasional, national and international, regional and global. Border control has multiplied and shifted; it has been technologically modernized and converted into a control arrangement with a high level of complexity. In view of this development, it makes more sense to speak of border regimes as ensembles of mobility-regulating forms of intervention (both facilitating and restricting mobility), rather than simply classic boom-gate borders. The new arrangements associated with these regimes move away from the container spaces of sovereign territories – not in the sense that these are dissolved or replaced, but that new forms of interconnectedness, overlap and extramural control emerge. The clarity and territorial coherence of the compartmental model are thus lost, and the distinction between national and global becomes blurred. At the same time, this nullifies certain typical characteristics of the classic nation-state 'container': the fixing of a territorial border and the binary coding of inside and outside. The new borders not only reproduce national territorial spaces, but also create new spaces. Border policies are still – though in a different way – concerned with modes of social sorting, which impose a spatial order and selectively facilitate, manage and prevent the circulation of people.

Expanding on this idea of the metamorphosis of borders, I have attempted to show that globalization itself is a thoroughly divided process, and that borders as sorting machines play a prominent role in this bifurcation. The participatory promise of globalization for all is not fulfilled, and it would be more accurate to speak of polarizing experiences of the border. Borders are the most important agents and infrastructures in the allocation of unequal opportunities for mobility, and mobility is directly linked to the operating performance of borders. It is this that determines who will enter, who will cross the border, who will be checked and who will be excluded from the territory. The technological features of the border are set up in such a way that they reinforce both its functions: stopping people and letting them pass through. The aim is to ensure that desirable travellers can slip over the border quickly, easily and comfortably, almost without noticing (in keeping with a concept associated with globalization, that of 'hyper-mobility'), while making border crossings impossible for undesirable travellers. It is only when mobility is effectively coded – as low-risk, desirable, valuable and economically profitable circulation on the one hand, and undesirable, high-risk circulation on the other – that borders can be made more permeable and border crossings streamlined. If borders do an accurate job of filtering, then the section of the earth's population that enjoys increasing mobility will see them as more open, and in fact will barely be able to see them or their closing function at all, while the rest of the world will perceive them as all the more limiting. Of course, one might object that this has always been the function of the border. But some aspects at least are new: first, the manner in which this function is made operable and, second, the spatial and social depth of the interventions that can be achieved with the new border regimes. The border as a filter does not operate solely at the edge of the territorial state, but combs through databases, delegates control, displaces the site of control, stores biometric data, uses the services of private companies and other states, and invests in new technologies.

In simple but striking terms, we could say that the old border was a 'people border' (*Personengrenze*). It operationalized selective entry, but – by and large – subjected everyone to the same level of control. The new border is an individualized border, distinguishing between different 'border people' (*Grenzpersonen*).[4] The growth in information, biometric recognition, pre-screening procedures and interoperable database systems is intended to guarantee that those people classified as high risk or undesirable are targeted and filtered out, without slowing down the flow of all the others (the minority, to be more precise). An even more far-reaching development is the 'expansion of the border zone': here, control and barrier effects move away from the border into the countries of origin and transit, and contribute to immobilizing people in the place where they live or are staying. By integrating third parties into their efforts at control, monitoring and migration prevention, some states create a *cordon sanitaire* thousands of kilometres from their actual national border.

In light of the above discussion, we can identify four overarching trends that are linked with the emergence of the new border regimes and are characteristic of these regimes.

The securitization of mobility

The concept of security established by the new border regimes operates on the basis of a central distinction: between trustworthy/low risk on the one hand and non-trustworthy/high risk on the other. The specific definition and elaboration of these categories is variable, however. The attributes regarded as risks prove to be contingent and highly susceptible to political manipulation. And since the border itself can be presented as a protective barrier against a complex, threatening, out-of-control and risky world, parts of the population see the hardening of borders, strict control and selectivity as desirable. Thanks to the 9/11 attacks and other cross-border terrorist activities, the threat from outside has become a fixed element of forms of social consciousness and has been subjected to corresponding political treatment. Likewise, in countries with substantial numbers of migrants (but also elsewhere), the fear of irregular and 'uncontrolled' immigration has contributed to a situation where trust in travellers' good intentions has been replaced by securitized travel. As we have known since the Covid pandemic (if not before), the security issue can be continually revitalized with new concerns, including health-related matters. There is a constantly updated rhetoric of security, which keeps recoding the border to strengthen its defences against external risks.[5] The concept of security now embedded in the border regimes is manifested in a whole ensemble of practices and technologies of control, following the script of the 'culture of suspicion'.[6] The border has thus become part of a prevention-oriented risk policy, which anticipates dangers and takes corresponding countermeasures.

Present-day architectures of border control combine the administrative act of control with preventive measures, algorithmic investigative work and predictions of probability. Just as a real-time virus scanner inspects data traffic for malware and suspicious actions, so the border as a 'semipermeable filter' is constantly working to find suspicious, high-risk and undesirable groups and individuals, and to exclude them from cross-border traffic or subject them to particularly attentive checks and examinations. If the minimization of risks and the production of security become the guiding principles of border policy, then comprehensive rights of free movement and mobility for all inevitably take a back seat.

Overlapping spaces of control

In the configuration described above, the control of mobility is not a matter that is restricted to the borderline. The border checkpoint, located right at the edge of the territory, has not necessarily lost its function, but a comprehensive and spatially diffused control regime has sprung up around it. This regime records, observes, monitors and controls people's movements, both digitally and physically. On the one hand, it uses technologies of control that are recognizable as checkpoints passed during individual journeys – at booths or border huts, gates, stations and crossings where permission is given for entry. On the other hand, it uses technologies that the controlled subjects are unaware of, either the 'surplus of control' arising from the daily use of digital devices, or the utilization of identifying and classifying technologies in public spaces. These 'bouncers' and controlling interventions are no longer found solely on entry to the territory, but in many different places. They feature ever more complex architectures of security, and merge private and governmental forms of control.

The new control activities are not always easy to detect, especially when we are dealing with control without personal collaboration, when public spaces are observed or data is accessed and analysed without consent. The surveillance of spaces and excessive data extraction can become a substitute for fixed borders, since they allow control even long after people have crossed the border into the territory, or long before they have reached it. One does not have to subscribe to a critical cultural analysis to see that digitization has substantial potential for control (much of which has yet to be fully exploited), and can easily be used to monitor mobility. Scanning, checking and tracing are no longer bound to either a place (the territorial border) or a controlling authority (the organs of the executive); instead, these are flexible, interconnected arrangements comprising control of and intervention in mobility. From this perspective, globalization is neither a de-spatialized nor an atopian project; instead, it leads to a situation where different spaces are embedded in and entangled with one another, and control is diffused. Nonetheless, the territorial border remains a central reference of these practices of control: even new places and levels of control, the 'border outside the border' and the 'border inside the border', all refer to the question of whether a person is permitted to be present in a territory, and what rights of mobility should be accorded.

Graduated rights

Even historically, mobility rights have never been the rights of equals, but have usually been attached to people's status. Safe conduct, the gate swinging open, the boom barrier rising: these have often been experiences reserved to a privileged few. Ultimately, the same is still true today. Globalization, however, has led from a fragmented patchwork to a steeply graduated, polarized and globally integrated system of unequal opportunities for mobility. This is important because our society views mobility as desirable, and more and more groups aspire to it. In a stationary society, where most people remain in the same place and border crossings are more the exception than the rule, unequal rights to mobility are less likely to cause friction. But in a globalized and mobilized society, where tourism, periods spent abroad, transnational social spaces and flexible practices of residence and transit are the norm, the question of what rights a person has to cross borders is becoming more and more important. The concept of 'mobility citizenship'[7] refers to the nexus of status and mobility rights. It highlights the fact that having the option to leave one's own territory, to cross borders, and to spend a short or long period of time elsewhere is just as much part of the catalogue of citizenship rights as access to social benefits or the right to vote. It should have become clear from what I have said so far that rights to mobility, today, are mainly conferred by possession of a citizenship, but that a person's economic resources (e.g., financial or human capital) also play a part. Access to greater freedom of movement is one of the key reasons why people give up their (previous) citizenship and apply for a new one – be it wealthy oligarchs buying 'golden passports', or the descendants of migrants. At the same time, more and more people are living in uncertain 'grey areas', in irregular situations without a fixed status or residence permit, and with only rudimentary rights. Prison-like camps make the state of emergency permanent and restrict the right to free movement, often for months or even years. Here the extremes of globalization – the bright side and the dark side – confront each other head on.

More recent developments suggest that uniform rights attached to a single citizenship may not be the end point of current changes. Government agencies, airlines and tech companies are working on increasingly refined security technologies, which are intended to allow individualized risk classifications for travellers. Thanks to enhanced capabilities for data storage, identification and targeted control, the classificatory ambitions of the agents of control are growing, and they are no longer willing to be satisfied with a mere passport. If, instead of just checking passports, they also have access to data on consumption, movement and social media behaviour, then they do not have to make do with generalized classifications, but can use scoring procedures to make individualized evaluations. Forms of algorithmic regulation arise when this data is used to make automated decisions and to set up permanent monitoring systems.[8]

In this world of the future, the social figure of the 'trusted traveller' (already featured in individual programmes) represents those who can be given extended mobility rights and permitted to cross borders easily because of the characteristics ascribed to them – risk profile, previous travel behaviour, economic power. The trusted traveller does not arise from a generalized, pre-existing trust, nor from approval on the basis of citizenship, but from the compilation and algorithmic analysis of behavioural data. People who enrol in 'trusted traveller' programmes in advance and obtain a high 'trust score' are granted a particularly high mobility status. In return for disclosing personal data, they are promised the use of streamlined passenger processing, so they can bypass the normal queues. Comfort and speed are guaranteed. In tandem with this development, the smartification of borders continues to gain ground, an insidious process bringing together new biometric data collection systems, large data repositories, and algorithmic classification processes. More and more often, visa applications are rejected or entry is denied at the border as the result of algorithmic selection processes, which mark out people with certain combinations of features as risks.

A global hierarchy

The traditional view of borders is concerned with territorial sovereignty and control and the regulation of entry and exit – in short, with the container state. In the first instance this is not a hierarchic structure, but assumes the parallel existence of nation-state compartments. This has also been understood as a horizontal segmentation of global society. From my perspective, borders are not just barriers, circuit-breakers or 'interrupters of interdependence' in the exchange between states; they are also thresholds of inequality in a global context. Not only can they consolidate and reproduce disparities between neighbouring countries, they also create – in combination with graduated rights – global hierarchies of different groups and affiliations. The border as a sorting machine is a generator of inequality like no other. At present, as stated above, there is a diametric opposition between the way the border is experienced by mobile and welcome travellers – privileged citizens of the Western world, the holders of 'power passports', people with high levels of human capital, and the global elite with the greatest wealth and the highest incomes – and the way it is experienced by the 'peripheral', the unwelcome and the excluded. While the first group is able to rhapsodize about a borderless world of free movement, the second group is faced with firmly closed borders. A global hierarchy of inequality emerges. Zygmunt Bauman, the diagnostician of globalized modernity, encapsulated these double standards of globalization in the following inimitable phrase: 'Some inhabit the globe; others are chained to place.'[9] The cosmopolitan tourist and the irregular migrant imprisoned in a camp are ultimately the two inextricably linked faces of globalization. The globalization of opening and closing, mobility and immobility must be understood in their causal connectedness.

There is no doubt that the globalized world is still a world of borders: not just a world of walls and fences, but also a world where control is multiplied. Despite repeated prognoses from the high priests of globalization, the border is not yet ready for its last rites – this was an illusion at the expense of third parties, for whom globalization means a hardening and not a dissolution of borders. In any case, the public reactions to the Covid-related border closures showed very strikingly that Western societies have internalized the narrative of debordering to such an extent that the 'return of borders' inevitably seemed like a moment of deglobalization. Few saw it for what it was: the repressed Other of a globalization in which the price of greater freedom of movement for some is reduced mobility for others. Borders as sorting machines are not relics of the past, but highly versatile and adaptable institutions, which can have a massive impact on individual options in life and on the world as a whole, today and most likely in the future. A universalization of the project of debordering is not in sight.

Notes

Chapter 1: Borders Are Back!

1   Cf. Markus Schroer, 'Grenzverhältnisse', *Soziopolis* (2016). https://www.soziopolis.de/beobachten/raum/artikel/grenzverhaeltnisse/.

2   Axel Dreher, Noel Gaston and Pim Martens, *Measuring Globalisation: Gauging Its Consequences*, New York: Springer Science+Business Media, 2008.

3   Hilary French, *Vanishing Borders: Protecting the Planet in the Age of Globalization*, New York: W. W. Norton, 2000.

4   Kenichi Ohmae, *The Borderless World*, London: Harper Collins, 1990.

5   Anthony Giddens, *The Consequences of Modernity*, Stanford: Stanford University Press, 1990.

6   Steffen Mau, *Social Transnationalism. Lifeworlds Beyond The Nation-State*, New York: Routledge, 2010.

7   Helmut Willke, *Atopia: Studien zur atopischen Gesellschaft*, Frankfurt am Main: Suhrkamp, 2001.

8   Craig Calhoun, 'The Class Consciousness of Frequent Travellers: Towards a Critique of Actually Existing Cosmopolitanism', in Daniele Archibugi (ed.), *Debating Cosmopolitics*, London: Verso, 2003, pp. 86–116.

9   Georg Simmel, 'Brücke und Tür', in *Das Individuum und die Freiheit: Essais*, Frankfurt am Main: Fischer, 1993 [1909], p. 7.

10 Thomas Nail, *Theory of the Border*, Oxford: Oxford University Press, 2016, p. 3.

11 For a similar argument, see Stephan Lessenich, *Neben uns die Sintflut: Die Externalisierungsgesellschaft und ihr Preis*, Munich: Hanser Berlin, 2016, pp. 48ff.; the beginnings of such an understanding, however, can already be found in Giddens, *The Consequences of Modernity*.

12 Matthew Longo, *The Politics of Borders: Sovereignty, Security, and the Citizen after 9/11*, Cambridge: Cambridge University Press, 2017, p. 5.

Chapter 2: Statehood, Territoriality and Border Control

1 Karl Schlögel, *Das sowjetische Jahrhundert: Archäologie einer untergegangenen Welt*, Munich: C. H. Beck, 2018.

2 Georg Jellinek, *Allgemeine Staatslehre*, Berlin: Springer, 1929.

3 Saskia Sassen, *Territory, Authority, Rights: From Medieval to Global Assemblages*, Princeton: Princeton University Press, 2008.

4 Robert D. Sack, 'Human Territoriality: A Theory', *Annals of the Association of American Geographers*, 73/1 (1983), pp. 55–74.

5 Stein Rokkan, *Staat, Nation und Demokratie in Europa*, Frankfurt am Main: Suhrkamp, 2000.

6 Peter Sahlins, *Boundaries: The Making of France and Spain in the Pyrenees*, Berkeley: University of California Press, 1989.

7 Rokkan, *Staat, Nation und Demokratie in Europa*.

8 Rogers Brubaker, *Citizenship and Nationhood in France and Germany*, Cambridge, MA: Harvard University Press, 1992.

9 Jürgen Mackert, 'Staatsbürgerschaft: Die Mechanismen interner Schließung', in Jürgen Mackert (ed.), *Die Theorie sozialer Schließung: Tradition, Analysen, Perspektiven*, Wiesbaden: VS Verlag für Sozialwissenschaften, 2004, p. 258.

10 Anthony Asiwaju, *Partitioned Africans: Ethnic Relations across Africa's International Boundaries 1884–1984*, London: Hurst, 1985.

11 Elliott Green, 'On the Size and Shape of African States', *International Studies Quarterly*, 56/2 (2012), pp. 229–244.

12 Jeffrey Herbst, 'The Creation and Maintenance of National Boundaries in Africa', *International Organization*, 43/4 (1989), pp. 673–692.

13 Michel Foucher, 'African Borders: Putting Paid to a Myth', *Journal of Borderlands Studies*, 35/2 (2020), pp. 287–306.

14 Boaz Atzili, *Good Fences, Bad Neighbors: Border Fixity and International Conflict*, Chicago: University of Chicago Press, 2012.

15 Atzili, *Good Fences, Bad Neighbors*.

16 Brian T. Sumner, 'Territorial Disputes at the International Court of Justice', *Duke Law Journal*, 53/6 (2003), pp. 1779–1812.

17 Alexander B. Murphy, 'Historical Justifications for Territorial Claims', *Annals of the Association of American Geographers*, 80/4 (1990), pp. 531–548.

18 This is, in any case, a key proposition of the major study on the history of the border by Alexander Demandt, *Grenzen: Geschichte und Gegenwart*, Berlin: Propyläen, 2020.

19 Jürgen Habermas, *The Postnational Constellation*, trans., ed. and intro. by Max Pensky, Cambridge: Polity, 2001, p. 67.

20 John Torpey, 'Coming and Going: On the State Monopolization of the Legitimate "Means of Movement"', *Sociological Theory*, 13/3 (1998), pp. 239–259.

21 Aristide R. Zolberg, 'The Exit Revolution', in Nancy L. Green and Francois Weil (eds.), *Citizenship and Those Who Leave: The Politics of Emigration and Expatriation* (Urbana: University of Illinois Press, 2007), pp. 33–60.

22 Andreas Fahrmeir, Oliver Faron and Patrick Weil (eds.), *Migration Control in the North Atlantic World: The Evolution of State Practices in Europe and the United States from the French Revolution to the Inter-War Period*, Providence: Berghahn, 2003; Sebastian Conrad, 'Globalization Effects: Mobility and Nation in Imperial Germany, 1880–1914', *Journal of Global History*, 3/1 (2008), pp. 43–66.

23 Gérard Noiriel, *Die Tyrannei des Nationalen: Sozialgeschichte des Asylrechts in Europa*, Luneburg: Klampen, 1994.

24 Simon A. Cole, *Suspect Identities: A History of Fingerprinting and Criminal Identification*, Cambridge, MA: Harvard University Press, 2001; Aristide R. Zolberg, 'Global Movements, Global Walls. Responses to Migration, 1885–1925', Gungwu Wang (ed.), *Global History and Migrations*, Boulder: Westview Press, 1997, pp. 279–307.

25 Torpey, 'Coming and Going'.

26 Stefan Zweig, *The World of Yesterday*, trans. Benjamin W. Huebsch and Helmut Ripperger, Lexington: Plunkett Lake Press, 2011, p. 90.

27 Conrad, 'Globalization Effects', p. 44.

28 Conrad, 'Globalization Effects', p. 47.

29 Stefan Kaufmann, 'Grenzregimes im Zeitalter globaler Netzwerke', in Helmuth Berking (ed.), *Die Macht des Lokalen in einer Welt ohne Grenzen*, Frankfurt am Main: Campus, 2006, pp. 32–65, here p. 42 (my translation).

30 Torpey, 'Coming and Going'.

31 Christoph Möllers, *Freiheitsgrade. Elemente einer liberalen politischen Mechanik*, Berlin: Suhrkamp, 2020, p. 142.

32 Daniel Drewski and Jürgen Gerhards, 'The Liberal Border Script and its Contestations: An Attempt of Definition and Systematization', SCRIPTS Working Paper, 4 (2020).

33 Malcolm Anderson, 'The Transformation of Border Controls: A European Precedent?', in Peter Andreas and Timothy Snyder (eds.), *The Wall around the West: State Borders and Immigration Controls in North America and Europe*, Lanham: Rowman & Littlefield, 2000, pp. 15–29, here p. 24.

34 Joseph H. Carens, 'Aliens and Citizens: The Case for Open Borders', *The Review of Politics*, 49/2 (1987), pp. 251–273.

Chapter 3: Opening and Closing: The Dialectic of Globalization

1 David Held, Anthony G. McGrew, David Goldblatt and Jonathan Perraton, *Global Transformations: Politics, Economics and Culture*, Stanford: Stanford University Press, 1999.

2 Andreas Wimmer and Nina Glick-Schiller, 'Methodological Nationalism and Beyond: Nation-State Building, Migration and the Social Sciences', *Global Networks*, 2/4 (2002), pp. 301–334.

3 Anthony Giddens, *The Consequences of Modernity*, Stanford: Stanford University Press, 1990, p. 64.

4 An overview is provided in Steffen Mau, *Social Transnationalism. Lifeworlds Beyond The Nation-State*, New York: Routledge, 2010; see also Anja Weiß, *Soziologie globaler Ungleichheiten*, Berlin: Suhrkamp, 2017.

5 Manuela Boatcă, *Global Inequalities Beyond Occidentalism*, Farnham: Ashgate, 2015.

6 John Urry, *The Tourist Gaze*, London: Sage Publications, 2001; John Urry, *Sociology Beyond Societies: Mobilities for the Twenty-First Century*, London: Routledge, 2000.

7 Axel Dreher, Noel Gaston and Pim Martens, *Measuring*

   Globalisation: Gauging Its Consequences, New York: Springer Science+Business Media, 2008.

8 See also Michael Zürn, *Regieren Jenseits des Nationalstaats: Globalisierung und Denationalisierung als Chance*, Frankfurt am Main: Suhrkamp, 1998.

9 Sushma Shukla, 'Covid-19 and Globalization: An Analysis', *Cape Comorin*, 2/4 (2020), https://www.researchgate.net /publication/341447744_COVID-19_and_Globalization_An _Analysis.

10 Elisabeth Noelle and Erich Peter Neumann (eds.), *Jahrbuch der Öffentlichen Meinung der Bundesrepublik 1947–1955*, Allensbach: Verlag für Demoskopie, 1956.

11 Mau, *Social Transnationalism*.

12 Markus Schroer, *Räume, Orte, Grenzen: Auf dem Weg zu einer Soziologie des Raumes*, Frankfurt am Main: Suhrkamp, 2006, p. 27.

13 Thomas L. Friedman, *The World Is Flat: A Brief History of the Twenty-First Century*, New York: Farrar, Straus and Giroux, 2006.

14 Mike Moore, *A World without Walls: Freedom, Development, Free Trade and Global Governance*, Cambridge: Cambridge University Press, 2003.

15 Saskia Sassen, *Losing Control? Sovereignty in the Age of Globalization*, New York: Columbia University Press, 1996.

16 Jürgen Habermas, *The Postnational Constellation*, trans., ed. and intro. by Max Pensky, Cambridge: Polity, 2001, p. 67.

17 Wayne A. Cornelius, Philip L. Martin and James F. Hollifield (eds.), *Controlling Immigration. A Global Perspective*, Stanford: Stanford University Press, 1994; Sassen, *Losing Control?*; Jagdish Bhagwati, 'Borders Beyond Control', *Foreign Affairs*, 82/1 (2003), pp. 98–104; Stephen Castles, 'Why Migration Policies Fail', *Ethnic and Racial Studies*, 27/2 (2004), pp. 205–227.

18 Bhagwati, 'Borders Beyond Control'.

19 Bhagwati, 'Borders Beyond Control', p. 22.

20 Wendy Brown, *Walled States, Waning Sovereignty*, New York: Zone Books, 2010.

21 Jan Eckel, 'Alles hängt mit allem zusammen: Zur Historisierung des Globalisierungsdiskurses der 1990er und 2000er Jahre', *Historische Zeitschrift*, 307/1 (2018), pp. 42–78.

22 Lorenzo Gabrielli, Emanuel Deutschmann, Fabrizio Natale, Ettore Recchi and Michele Vespe, 'Dissecting Global Air Traffic Data to Discern Different Types and Trends of Transnational Human Mobility', *EPJ Data Science*, 8/1 (2019), pp. 1–24.

23 Dirk Glaesser, John Kester, Hanna Paulose, Abbas Alizadeh and Birka Valentin, 'Global Travel Patterns: An Overview', *Journal of Travel Medicine*, 24/4 (2017).

24 UNWTO International Tourism Organization, *International Tourism Highlights*, Madrid: UNWTO, 2019, p. 15.

25 Sources: https://www.ambodenbleiben.de/hintergrund/zahlen -und-fakten/ and https://www.zeit.de/wissen/umwelt/2019-05 /flugverzicht-klimapolitik-emissionen-verantwortung-privileg.

26 Peter Andreas and Timothy Snyder (eds.), *The Wall around the West: State Borders and Immigration Controls in North America and Europe*, Lanham: Rowman & Littlefield, 2000.

27 Brown, *Walled States, Waning Sovereignty*.

28 Cf. also Stephan Lessenich, *Neben uns die Sintflut: Die Externalisierungsgesellschaft und ihr Preis*, Munich: Hanser Berlin, 2016, p. 125.

29 E.g., Stephen Castles, 'Hierarchical Citizenship in a World of Unequal Nation-States', *PS: Political Science and Politics* 38/4 (2005), pp. 689 –692; Mathias Czaika and Hein De Haas, 'The Globalization of Migration: Has the World Become More Migratory?', *International Migration Review* 48/2 (2014), pp. 283–323.

30 Ronen Shamir, 'Without Borders? Notes on Globalization as a Mobility Regime', *Sociological Theory* 23/2 (2005), pp. 197–217; Steffen Mau, Heike Brabandt, Lena Laube and Christof Roos, *Liberal States and the Freedom of Movement: Selective Borders, Unequal Mobility*, Basingstoke: Palgrave Macmillan, 2012.

31 Zygmunt Bauman, 'On Glocalization: Or Globalization for Some, Localization for Others', *Thesis Eleven*, 54/1 (1998), p. 45.

32 Giddens, *The Consequences of Modernity*; see also Lessenich, *Neben uns die Sintflut*, p. 48.

33 A similar argument is put forward by Ronen Shamir, who states that the literature of globalization has overtheorized openness and undertheorized closure. See Shamir, 'Without Borders?', p. 197.

Chapter 4: Fortification: Border Walls as Bulwarks of Globalization

1 Stéphane Rosière and Reece Jones, 'Teichopolitics: Re-Considering Globalisation through the Role of Walls and Fences', *Geopolitics*, 17/1 (2012), pp. 217–234.

2 Ron E. Hassner and Jason Wittenberg, 'Barriers to Entry: Who

Builds Fortified Boundaries and Why?', *International Security*, 40/1 (2015), pp. 157–190.

3 Élisabeth Vallet, 'State of Border Walls in a Globalized World', Andréanne Bisonette and Élisabeth Vallet (eds.), *Borders and Border Walls: In-Security, Symbolism, Vulnerabilities*, London: Routledge, 2021, pp. 7–24; Élisabeth Vallet (ed.), *Borders, Fences and Walls: State of Insecurity?*, London: Routledge, 2016.

4 Nazli Avdan, *Visas and Walls: Border Security in the Age of Terrorism*, Philadelphia: University of Pennsylvania Press, 2019.

5 Reece Jones and Corey Johnson, 'Border Militarisation and the Re-articulation of Sovereignty', *Transactions of the Institute of British Geographers*, 41/2 (2016), pp. 187–200.

6 Jones and Johnson, 'Border Militarisation and the Re-articulation of Sovereignty', p. 196.

7 Funded by the German Research Foundation (DFG) in the framework of the Collaborative Research Centre 'Re-Figuration of Spaces' (project number 290045248–SFB 1265).

8 Vallet, 'State of Border Walls in a Globalized World', p. 10.

9 Markus Schroer, *Räume der Gesellschaft: Soziologische Studien*, Wiesbaden: Springer, 2019), p. 260.

10 Derek S. Denman, 'On Fortification: Military Architecture, Geometric Power, and Defensive Design', *Security Dialogue*, 51/2–3 (2020), pp. 231–247, here p. 233.

11 Avdan, *Visas and Walls*.

12 Peter Andreas, 'Redrawing the Line: Borders and Security in the Twenty-First Century', *International Security*, 28/2 (2003), pp. 78–111.

13 Vallet, 'State of Border Walls in a Globalized World', p. 11.

14 https://grist.org/article/napolitano-knows/.

15 Reece Jones, 'The Poetry of "Build the Wall"', *Journal of Latin American Geography*, 17/3 (2018), pp. 254–255.

16 Nazli Avdan and Christopher F. Gelpi, 'Do Good Fences Make Good Neighbors? Border Barriers and the Transnational Flow of Terrorist Violence', *International Studies Quarterly*, 61/1 (2017), pp. 14–27.

17 Steffen Mau, 'Mobility Citizenship, Inequality, and the Liberal State: The Case of Visa Policies', *International Political Sociology*, 4/4 (2010), pp. 339–361; Steffen Mau and Heike Brabandt, 'Visumpolitik und die Regulierung globaler Mobilität', *Zeitschrift für Soziologie*, 40/1 (2011); Steffen Mau, Fabian Gülzau and Kristina Korte, 'Grenzen

erkunden: Grenzinfrastrukturen und die Rolle fortifizierter Grenzen im globalen Kontext', in Martina Löw, Volkan Sayman, Jona Schwerer and Hannah Wolf (eds.), *Am Ende der Globalisierung: Über die Re-Figuration von Räumen*, Bielefeld: transcript, 2021, pp. 129–152.

18   Hassner and Wittenberg, 'Barriers to Entry'.

19   Fabian Gülzau and Steffen Mau, 'Walls, Barriers, Checkpoints, and Landmarks: A Quantitative Typology of Border Control Infrastructures', *Historical Social Research*, 46/3 (2021), pp. 23–48.

20   Rosière and Jones, 'Teichopolitics: Re-Considering Globalisation through the Role of Walls and Fences', p. 217.

21   David B. Carter and Paul Poast, 'Why Do States Build Walls? Political Economy, Security, and Border Stability', *Journal of Conflict Resolution*, 61/2 (2017), pp. 239–270.

22   Carter and Poast, 'Why Do States Build Walls?', p. 263.

23   Ulrich Beck, *Die Neuvermessung der Ungleichheit unter den Menschen: Soziologische Aufklärung im 21. Jahrhundert*, Frankfurt am Main: Suhrkamp, 2008.

24   We use this term in CRC 1265, 'Re-Figuration of Spaces': see Martina Löw and Hubert Knoblauch, 'Die Re-Figuration von Räumen', SFB 1265 Working Paper, 1 (2019).

25   Kristina Korte, '"Who Is the Animal in the Zoo?" Fencing In and Fencing Out at the Hungarian-Serbian Border: A Qualitative Case Study', *Journal of Borderlands Studies*, (2020), pp. 1–22.

26   Korte, '"Who Is the Animal in the Zoo?"'.

27   Beth A. Simmons and Michael Kenwick, 'Border Orientation in a Globalizing World: Concept and Measurement' (2019), http://dx.doi.org/10.2139/ssrn.3326773.

28   Denman, 'On Fortification'.

29   Reece Jones, *Border Walls: Security and the War on Terror in the United States, India, and Israel*, London, New York: Zed Books, 2012.

30   Wendy Brown, *Walled States, Waning Sovereignty*, New York: Zone Books, 2010.

31   Katharina Inhetveen, *Die Politische Ordnung des Flüchtlingslagers: Akteure-Macht-Organisation. Eine Ethnographie im südlichen Afrika*, Bielefeld: transcript, 2010.

32   Giorgio Agamben, *Homo Sacer*, Frankfurt am Main: Suhrkamp, 2002.

33   Inhetveen, *Die Politische Ordnung des Flüchtlingslagers*; Anna Marie Steigemann and Philipp Misselwitz, 'Architectures of

Asylum: Making Home in a State of Permanent Temporariness',
Current Sociology, 68/5 (2020), pp. 628–650.

Chapter 5: Filtering Borders: Granting Unequal Opportunities for Mobility

1 These two examples are taken from Steffen Mau, 'Unsichtbare Grenzen', *Die ZEIT*, 26 June 2008, p. 11.
2 https://www.derstandard.at/story/2000117194363/ohne-impfpass-kein-grenzuebertritt-wie-corona-grenzen-mililtarisiert.
3 Cindy Cheng, Joan Barcelo, Allison S. Hartnett, Robert Kubinec and Luca Messerschmidt, 'Covid-19 Government Response Event Dataset (Coronanet V.1.0)', *Nature Human Behaviour*, 4/7 (2020), pp. 756–768.
4 Neil M. Ferguson, Derek A. T. Cummings, Christophe Fraser, James C. Cajka, Philip C. Cooley and Donald S. Burke, 'Strategies for Mitigating an Influenza Pandemic', *Nature*, 442/7101 (2006), pp. 448–452.
5 Ruud Koopmans, 'A Virus That Knows No Borders? Exposure to and Restrictions of International Travel and the Global Diffusion of Covid-19', WZB Discussion Paper, SP VI 2020–103 (2020).
6 Beth A. Simmons and Michael Kenwick, 'Border Orientation in a Globalizing World: Concept and Measurement' (2019), http://dx.doi.org/10.2139/ssrn.3326773.
7 Lucy Budd, Morag Bell and Tim Brown, 'Of Plagues, Planes and Politics: Controlling the Global Spread of Infectious Diseases by Air', *Political Geography*, 28/7 (2009), pp. 426–435.
8 Famous images from Ellis Island show recently landed immigrants, just a stone's throw from the Statue of Liberty, standing in a long line to be examined by health inspectors, who checked that they had no communicable diseases and were fit to immigrate to the US. People diagnosed with diseases during the crossing or while waiting for entry were taken to the artificial quarantine islands, Swinburne Island and Hoffman Island. It is probably no coincidence that the opening of luggage, searches through clothing and body searches bear similarities to medical examinations, which are concerned with the body and vital functions.
9 Alison Bashford, 'At the Border: Contagion, Immigration,

Nation', *Australian Historical Studies*, 33/120 (2002), pp. 344–358.

10 Bashford, 'At the Border'; Alison Bashford (ed.), *Medicine at the Border: Disease, Globalization and Security, 1850 to the Present*, Basingstoke, New York: Palgrave Macmillan, 2007.

11 Andreas Reckwitz, 'Risikopolitik', in Michael Volkmer and Karin Werner (eds.), *Die Corona-Gesellschaft: Analysen zur Lage und Perspektiven für die Zukunft*, Bielefeld: transcript, 2020, pp. 242–251.

12 Ulrich Beck, *Weltrisikogesellschaft: Auf der Suche nach der verlorenen Sicherheit*, Frankfurt am Main: Suhrkamp, 2007.

13 Barry Buzan, Ole Wæver and Jaap De Wilde, *Security: A New Framework for Analysis*, Boulder: Lynne Rienner Publishers, 1998.

14 Nina Amelung, Rafaela Granja and Helena Machado, *Modes of Bio-Bordering: The Hidden (Dis)Integration of Europe*, London: Springer Nature, 2021, p. 17.

15 Stephan Lessenich, *Neben uns die Sintflut: Die Externalisierungsgesellschaft und ihr Preis*, Munich: Hanser Berlin, 2016, p. 135.

16 Mark B. Salter, 'At the Threshold of Security. A Theory of International Borders', in Elia Zureik and Mark Salter, *Global Surveillance and Policing*, Cullompton: Willan, 2005, pp. 48–62.

17 Christian Joppke, 'Why Liberal States Accept Unwanted Immigration', *World Politics*, 50/2 (1998), pp. 266–293.

18 Alexander R. Hayes and Carolyn M. Dudek, 'How Radical Right-Wing Populism Has Shaped Recent Migration Policy in Austria and Germany', *Journal of Immigrant & Refugee Studies*, 18/2 (2020), pp. 133–150.

19 Marc Helbling and Dorina Kalkum, 'Migration Policy Trends in OECD Countries', *Journal of European Public Policy*, 25/12 (2018), pp. 1779–1797.

20 Michel Beine, Anna Boucher, Brian Burgoon, Mary Crock, Justin Gest, Michael Hiscox, Patrick McGovern, Hillel Rapoport, Joep Schaper and Eiko Thielemann, 'Comparing Immigration Policies: An Overview from the Impala Database', *International Migration Review*, 50/4 (2016), pp. 827–863.

21 https://taz.de/Erntehelfer-Fluege-aus-Rumaenien/!5675434/.

22 Ayelet Shachar, *The Birthright Lottery: Citizenship and Global Inequality*, Cambridge, MA: Harvard University Press, 2009.

23 Manuela Boatcă and Julia Roth, 'Unequal and Gendered: Notes on the Coloniality of Citizenship', *Current Sociology*, 64/2 (2016), pp. 191–212.

24 Branko Milanović, *Global Inequality. A New Approach for the Age of Globalization*, Cambridge, MA: Harvard University Press, 2016.

25 See Christian Joppke, *Neoliberal Nationalism: Immigration and the Rise of the Populist Right*, Cambridge: Cambridge University Press, 2021, Chapter 3.

26 Christian Joppke, 'Comparative Citizenship: A Restrictive Turn in Europe?', *Law & Ethics of Human Rights*, 2/1 (2008), pp. 1–41.

27 Kristin Surak, 'Global Citizenship 2.0. The Growth of Citizenship by Investment Programs', Investment Migration Paper, 03 (2016), p. 3.

28 https://www.bundestag.de/presse/hib/683118-683118.

29 Branko Milanović, *Capitalism, Alone: The Future of the System That Rules the World*, Cambridge, MA: Belknap Press, 2019, p. 134.

30 https://www.zeit.de/2020/49/goldene-paesse-eu-pass-malta -zykern-verkauf-organisierte-kriminalitaet.

31 https://www.zeit.de/2020/49/goldene-paesse-eu-pass-malta -zykern-verkauf-organisierte-kriminalitaet.

32 Aihwa Ong, *Flexible Citizenship. The Cultural Logics of Transnationality*, Durham, NC: Duke University Press, 1999.

33 Sara Kalm, 'Citizenship Capital', *Global Society*, 34/4 (2020), pp. 528–551.

34 http://www.henleyglobal.com/residence/overview/.

35 Manuela Boatcă, 'Karibische Überseegebiete: Der Kolonialismus ist nicht vorbei' (2020), https://mobile.katapult-magazin.de/ ?mpage=a&l=0&artID=1195.

36 Eric Neumayer, 'On the Detrimental Impact of Visa Restrictions on Bilateral Trade and Foreign Direct Investment', *Applied Geography*, 31/3 (2011), pp. 901–907.

37 Robert A. Lawson and Saurav Roychoudhury, 'Do Travel Visa Requirements Impede Tourist Travel?', *Journal of Economics and Finance*, 40/4 (2016), pp. 817–828.

38 Steffen Mau and Heike Brabandt, 'Visumpolitik und die Regulierung globaler Mobilität', *Zeitschrift für Soziologie*, 40/1 (2011); Steffen Mau, Fabian Gülzau, Lena Laube and Natascha Zaun, 'The Global Mobility Divide: How Visa Policies Have Evolved over Time', *Journal of Ethnic and Migration Studies*, 41/8 (2015), pp. 1192–1213.

39 UNWTO International Tourism Organization, *International Tourism Highlights*, Madrid: UNWTO, 2019, p. 4.

40 Mau et al., 'The Global Mobility Divide'.
41 UNWTO World Tourism Organization, *Visa Openness Report 2018*, Madrid: UNWTO, 2018.
42 Mau and Brabandt, 'Visumpolitik und die Regulierung globaler Mobilität', pp. 17ff.; Mathias Czaika, Hein de Haas and María Villares-Varela, 'The Global Evolution of Travel Visa Regimes', *Population and Development Review*, 44/3 (2018), pp. 589–622.
43 Mau and Brabandt, 'Visumpolitik und die Regulierung globaler Mobilität'; Steffen Mau, 'Mobility Citizenship, Inequality, and the Liberal State: The Case of Visa Policies', *International Political Sociology*, 4/4 (2010), pp. 339–361.
44 Jacob Thomas, 'When Political Freedom Does Not Offer Travel Freedom: The Varying Determinants of Visa-Free Travel Opportunities', *International Migration*, 58/2 (2020), pp. 80–97.
45 For this data see Ettore Recchi, Emanuel Deutschmann, Lorenzo Gabrielli and Nodira Kholmatova, 'The Global Visa Cost Divide: How and Why the Price for Travel Permits Varies Worldwide', *Political Geography* (2021), https://doi.org/10.1016/j.polgeo.2021.102350.
46 Recchi et al., 'The Global Visa Cost Divide', p. 5.
47 Mau, 'Mobility Citizenship, Inequality, and the Liberal State'. More recent data on Schengen visa rejection rates by country can be found at: https://ec.europa.eu/home-affairs/what-we-do/policies/borders-andvisas/visa-policy_en#stats.
48 Bertold Brecht, *Refugee Conversations*, trans. Romy Fursland, ed. and intro. by Tom Kuhn, London: Bloomsbury Publishing, 2020, p. 8.

Chapter 6: Smart Borders: Informational and Biometric Control

1 https://www.nytimes.com/2019/01/26/opinion/sunday/border-wallimmigration-trump.html.
2 Mark B. Salter, 'Passports, Mobility, and Security: How Smart Can the Border Be?', *International Studies Perspectives*, 5/1 (2004), pp. 71–91; Benjamin J. Muller, 'Unsafe at Any Speed? Borders, Mobility and "Safe Citizenship"', *Citizenship Studies*, 14/1 (2010), pp. 75–88.
3 Matthew Longo, *The Politics of Borders: Sovereignty, Security, and the Citizen after 9/11*, Cambridge: Cambridge University Press, 2017.

4   https://www.sueddeutsche.de/politik/brexit-irland-smart
    -border-backstop-1.4316547.

5   http://www.chinadaily.com.cn/a/202009/01
    /WS5f4deb99a310675eafc56cf7.html.

6   Régis Debray, *Lob der Grenzen* (Hamburg: Laika-Verlag,
    2016), p. 16.

7   https://www.sita.aero/pressroom/blog/enabling-the-european
    -entryexit-system/.

8   Ayelet Shachar, 'The Shifting Border: Legal Cartographies of
    Migration and Mobility', in *The Shifting Border*, Manchester:
    Manchester University Press, 2020, pp. 3–96, here p. 38.

9   In the context of the discussion about the politically contentious
    border between Ireland and Northern Ireland, and the question
    of how this border could function as the EU's external border
    without causing new unrest, the term 'Smart Border 2.0' has
    been evoked. Such a border could identify people and vehicles
    via barcodes or electromagnetic transponders attached to
    vehicles or integrated into driving licences or ID cards. People
    with such a device would then be able to cross the border more
    or less without hindrance. https://www.iata.org/contentassets/6
    faf144041864834820cc7963b2127ee/seamless-journey.pdf.

10 https://www.arabianbusiness.com/transport/406044-dubai
    -airporttrials-smart-tunnel-that-allows-passengers-clear
    -passport-control-in-15-seconds.

11 Ricky Wichum, *Biometrie: Zur Soziologie der Identifikation*,
    Paderborn: Wilhelm Fink, 2017.

12 Richard Jones, 'Checkpoint Security: Gateways, Airports and
    the Architecture of Security', in Katja Franko Aas, Helene
    Oppen Gundhus and Heidi Mork Lomell (eds.), *Technologies
    of Insecurity: The Surveillance of Everyday Life* (New York:
    Routledge-Cavendish, 2008), pp. 95–116; Polly Pallister-
    Wilkins, 'How Walls Do Work: Security Barriers as Devices
    of Interruption and Data Capture', *Security Dialogue*, 47/2
    (2016), pp. 151–164.

13 https://windsorstar.com/news/local-news/u-s-customs-to
    -collectdna-at-detroit-border-under-pilot-program.

14 Nina Amelung, Rafaela Granja and Helena Machado, *Modes
    of Bio-Bordering: The Hidden (Dis)Integration of Europe*,
    London: Springer Nature, 2021.

15 Steffen Mau, *The Metric Society: On the Quantification of the
    Social*, Cambridge: Polity, 2019.

16 Didier Bigo, 'Freedom and Speed in Enlarged Borderzones',
    in Vicki Squire (ed.), *The Contested Politics of Mobility:*

Borderzones and Irregularity, New York: Routledge, 2011, pp. 31–50.

17   Btihai Ajana, 'Augmented Borders: Big Data and the Ethics of Immigration Control', *Journal of Information, Communication and Ethics in Society*, 13/1 (2015), pp. 58–78.

18   Shoshana Zuboff, *The Age of Surveillance Capitalism: The Fight for a Human Future at the New Frontier of Power*, London: Profile Books, 2019.

19   https://www.hrw.org/news/2020/06/09/russias-latest-app-will-trackmigrant-workers-whos-next.

20   Louise Amoore, 'Biometric Borders: Governing Mobilities in the War on Terror', *Political Geography*, 25/3 (2006), pp. 336–351.

21   Deborah Lupton, *Data Selves: More-Than-Human Perspectives*, Cambridge: Polity, 2019.

22   Amoore, 'Biometric Borders'.

23   https://onezero.medium.com/clear-conquered-u-s-airports-now-itwants-to-own-your-entire-digital-identity-15d61076e44d.

24   Claudia Aradau and Tobias Blanke, 'Governing Others: Anomaly and the Algorithmic Subject of Security', *European Journal of International Security*, 3/1 (2018), pp. 1–21.

25   The global vaccine alliance GAVI has even developed a 'Covi-Pass' for West Africa in collaboration with Mastercard. https://dig.watch/updates/mastercard-and-truststamp-developing-covid-19-vaccination-identity.

26   https://www.iala.org/programs/passenger/travel-pass.

27   Freedom House, 'Freedom on the Net 2020. The Pandemic's Digital Shadow' (2020), https://freedomhouse.org/report/freedom-net/2020/pandemics-digital-shadow.

28   Petra Molnar, *Technological Testing Grounds: Migration Managements and Reflections from the Ground Up*, Refugee Law Lab 2020, https://edri.org/wp-content/uploads/2020/11/Technological-Testing-Grounds.pdf.

29   Conrad Ziller and Marc Helbling, 'Public Support for State Surveillance', *European Journal of Political Research*, 60/4 (2020), pp. 994–1006.

Chapter 7: Macroterritories: Dismantling Internal Borders, Upgrading External Borders

1   Krishan Kumar, *Empires: A Historical and Political Sociology*, Cambridge: Polity, 2020.

2   Sönke Neitzel, *Weltmacht oder Untergang: Die Weltreichslehre im Zeitalter des Imperialismus*, Paderborn, Munich: Schöningh, 2000.

3   Herfried Münkler, *Imperien: Die Logik der Weltherrschaft – vom Alten Rom bis zu den Vereinigten Staaten*, Berlin: Rowohlt, 2014.

4   Samuel P. Huntington, 'The Clash of Civilizations?', in Lane Crothers and Charles Lockhart (eds.), *Culture and Politics*, New York: Palgrave Macmillan, 2000, pp. 99–118.

5   Peter Andreas and Timothy Snyder (eds.), *The Wall around the West: State Borders and Immigration Controls in North America and Europe*, Lanham: Rowman & Littlefield, 2000.

6   Ron E. Hassner and Jason Wittenberg, 'Barriers to Entry: Who Builds Fortified Boundaries and Why?', *International Security*, 40/1 (2015), pp. 157–190.

7   Emanuel Deutschmann, *Mapping the Transnational World: How We Move and Communicate across Borders, and Why It Matters*, Princeton: Princeton University Press, 2022.

8   Fabian Gülzau, Steffen Mau and Natascha Zaun, 'Regional Mobility Spaces? Visa Waiver Policies and Regional Integration', *International Migration*, 54/6 (2016), pp. 164–180.

9   Ettore Recchi, *Mobile Europe: The Theory and Practice of Free Movement in the EU*, New York: Palgrave Macmillan, 2015; Jan Delhey, Emanuel Deutschmann, Monika Verbalyte and Auke Aplowski, *Netzwerk Europa: Wie ein Kontinent durch Mobilität und Kommunikation zusammenwächst*, Wiesbaden: Springer, 2020.

10 Fabian Gülzau, 'The "New Normal" for the Schengen Area: When, Where, and Why Member States Reintroduce Temporary Border Controls?', *Journal of Borderlands Studies*, 2021.

11 Gülzau, 'The "New Normal" for the Schengen Area'.

12 Steffen Mau, 'Die Politik der Grenze: Grenzziehung und politische Systembildung in der Europäischen Union', *Berliner Journal für Soziologie*, 1 (2006), pp. 123–140.

13 Lena Laube and Andreas Müller, 'Warum die Kontrolle abgeben? Die Delegation von Migrationskontrolle aus der Prinzipal-Agent-Perspektive', in: *Berliner Journal für Soziologie*, 25/3 (2015), pp. 255–281.

14 https://www.bbc.com/news/world-europe-51721356.

15 Nina Amelung, Rafaela Granja and Helena Machado, *Modes of Bio-Bordering: The Hidden (Dis)Integration of Europe*, London: Springer Nature, 2021.

16 IOM – International Organization for Migration, *Free*

Movement of Persons in Regional Integration Processes, Geneva: IOM, 2010.

17 IOM, 'Free Movement of Persons in Regional Integration Processes'; Vincet Hakyemez, 'The Visa System in International Relations: Patterns of Hierarchy, Reciprocity and Regionalization', *CISD Yearbook of Global Studies*, 1/1 (2014), pp. 11–28; Sonja Nita, 'Free Movement of People within Regional Integration Processes: A Comparative Perspective', in Sonja Nita, Antoine Pécoud, Philippe de Lombaerde, Kate Neyts and Joshua Gartland (eds.), *Migration, Free Movement and Regional Integration*, Paris: UNESCO, 2017, pp. 3–44.

18 Gülzau et al., 'Regional Mobility Spaces?'.

19 Gülzau et al., 'Regional Mobility Spaces?'.

20 Martha L. Cottam and Otwin Marcnin, 'The Management of Border Security in NAFTA: Imagery, Nationalism, and the War on Drugs', *International Criminal Justice Review*, 15/1 (2005), pp. 5–37; Anthony Minnaar, 'Border Control and Regionalism: The Case of South Africa', *African Security Review*, 10/2 (2001), pp. 89–102.

21 Cf. Andrew Geddes, Marcia Vera Espinoza, Leila Hadj Abdou and Leiza Brumat (eds.), *The Dynamics of Regional Migration Governance*, Cheltenham: Edward Elgar Publishing, 2019; Samuel Kehinde Okunade and Olusola Ogunnubi, 'A "Schengen" Agreement in Africa? African Agency and the ECOWAS Protocol on Free Movement', *Journal of Borderlands Studies*, (2021), pp. 119–137.

Chapter 8: Extraterritorializing Control: The Expansion of the Border Zone

1 Étienne Balibar, 'The Borders of Europe', in Pheng Cheah and Bruce Robbins (eds.), *Cosmopolitics. Thinking and Feeling Beyond the Nation* (Minneapolis: University of Minnesota Press, 1998), pp. 216–233.

2 This is the idea formulated by Ayelet Shachar in 'The Shifting Border: Legal Cartographies of Migration and Mobility', in *The Shifting Border*, Manchester: Manchester University Press, 2020, pp. 3–96, here p. 7.

3 Steffen Mau, Heike Brabandt, Lena Laube and Christof Roos, *Liberal States and the Freedom of Movement: Selective*

Borders, Unequal Mobility, London: Palgrave Macmillan, 2012.

4   Lena Laube, *Grenzkontrollen jenseits nationaler Territorien: Die Steuerung globaler Mobilität durch liberale Staaten*, Frankfurt am Main: Campus, 2013.

5   Shachar, 'The Shifting Border'.

6   Julia O'Connell Davidson, 'The Right to Locomotion? Trafficking, Slavery and the State', in Prabha Kotiswaran (eds.), *Revisiting the Law and Governance of Trafficking, Forced Labor and Modern Slavery*, Cambridge: Cambridge University Press, 2017, pp. 157–178.

7   Nira Yuval-Davis, Georgie Wemyss and Kathryn Cassidy, 'Everyday Bordering, Belonging and the Reorientation of British Immigration Legislation', *Sociology*, 52/2 (2018), pp. 228–244.

8   Laube, *Grenzkontrollen jenseits nationaler Territorien*. For similar systematic analyses, see also Dita Vogel, 'Migration Control in Germany and the United States', *International Migration Review*, 34/2 (2000), pp. 390–422; Maurizio Ambrosini and Anna Triandafyllidou, 'Irregular Immigration Control in Italy and Greece: Strong Fencing and Weak Gate-Keeping Serving the Labour Market', *European Journal of Migration and Law*, 13/3 (2011), pp. 251–273; Shachar, 'The Shifting Border'.

9   Shachar, 'The Shifting Border'.

10 Maartje Van der Woude, Vanessa Barker and Joanne van der Leun, *Crimmigration in Europe*, London: Sage, 2017.

11 Beth A. Simmons, Paulette Lloyd and Brandon M. Stewart, 'The Global Diffusion of Law: Transnational Crime and the Case of Human Trafficking', *International Organization*, 72/2 (2018), pp. 249–281.

12 Federica Infantino, 'State-bound Visa Policies and Europeanized Practices: Comparing EU Visa Policy Implementation in Marocco', *Journal of Borderland Studies*, 31/2 (2016), pp. 171–186.

13 Laube, *Grenzkontrollen jenseits nationaler Territorien*, p. 173.

14 Ruben Zaiotti (ed.), *Externalizing Migration Management: Europe, North America and the Spread of 'Remote Control' Practices*, London: Routledge, 2016.

15 Lena Laube, 'The Relational Dimension of Externalizing Border Control: Selective Visa Policies in Migration and Border Diplomacy', *Comparative Migration Studies*, 7/29 (2019), pp. 1–22.

16 Mau et al., *Liberal States and the Freedom of Movement*, pp. 100ff.

17 Jean-Pierre Cassarino, 'A Reappraisal of the EU's Expanding Readmission System', *The International Spectator*, 49/4 (2014), pp. 130–145, here p. 132.

18 Rahmane Idrissa, 'Dialog im Widerstreit: Folgewirkungen der EU-Migrationspolitik auf die Westafrikanische Integration. Dargestellt anhand der Fallbeispiele Nigeria, Mali und Niger', *Friedrich-Ebert-Stiftung* (2018), p. 33.

19 Inken Bartels, *Money against Migration: The EU Emergency Trust Fund for Africa*. Heinrich Böll Foundation 2019, https://www.boell.de/sites/default/files/money_against_migration.pdf.

20 Shachar, 'The Shifting Border'. In the following paragraphs, I largely follow my own argument in Ayelet Shachar's book; see Steffen Mau, 'Borders that Stay, Move, and Expand', in Ayelet Shachar (ed.), *The Shifting Border: Legal Cartographies of Migration and Mobility*, Manchester: Manchester University Press, 2020, pp. 140–158.

21 Tugba Basaran, 'Security, Law, Borders: Spaces of Exclusion', *International Political Sociology*, 2/4 (2008), pp. 339–354.

22 Shachar, 'The Shifting Border'.

23 Christian Joppke, 'Comparative Citizenship: A Restrictive Turn in Europe?', *Law & Ethics of Human Rights*, 2/1 (2008), pp. 1–41; James F. Hollifield, 'The Emerging Migration State', *International Migration Review*, 38/3 (2004), pp. 885–912.

Chapter 9: Globalized Borders

1 Hilary French, *Vanishing Borders: Protecting the Planet in the Age of Globalization*, New York: W. W. Norton, 2000.

2 Saskia Sassen, *Territory, Authority, Rights: From Medieval to Global Assemblages*, Princeton: Princeton University Press, 2008.

3 Aristide R. Zolberg, *A Nation by Design: Immigration Policy in the Fashioning of America*, New York: Russell Sage Foundation, 2006, p. 443.

4 See also Ayelet Shachar, 'The Shifting Border: Legal Cartographies of Migration and Mobility', in *The Shifting Border*, Manchester: Manchester University Press, 2020, pp. 3–96, here p. 35.

5 Jef Huysmans, 'The European Union and the Securitization of

Migration', *Journal of Common Market Studies*, 38/5 (2000), pp. 751–777.

6   Ronen Shamir, 'Without Borders? Notes on Globalization as a Mobility Regime', *Sociological Theory* 23/2 (2005), pp. 197–217.

7   John Urry, *Sociology Beyond Societies: Mobilities for the Twenty- First Century*, London: Routledge, 2000; Steffen Mau, 'Mobility Citizenship, Inequality, and the Liberal State: The Case of Visa Policies', *International Political Sociology*, 4/4 (2010), pp. 339–361.

8   Karen Yeung, 'Algorithmic Regulation: A Critical Interrogation', *Regulation & Governance*, 12/4 (2018), pp. 505–523.

9   Zygmunt Bauman, 'On Glocalization: Or Globalization for Some, Localization for Others', *Thesis Eleven*, 54/1 (1998), p. 45.

Index

Page numbers in *italics* refer to a table/figure